TAMING
THE FEAST
BEAST

RATIONAL RECOVERY

TAMING THE FEAST BEAST

How to Recognize the Voice of Fatness and End Your Struggle with Food Forever

Jack Trimpey, L.C.S.W, and Lois Trimpey, M.Ed.

Delacorte Press

Published by
Delacorte Press
Bantam Doubleday Dell Publishing Group, Inc.
1540 Broadway
New York, New York 10036

Grateful acknowledgment is made to Linda L. Millard for
use of her illustration on page 60.

Library of Congress Cataloging in Publication Data
Trimpey, Lois.
Taming the feast beast : how to recognize the voice of fatness and
end your struggle with food forever / Lois Trimpey and Jack
Trimpey.
p.   cm.
ISBN 0-385-31206-7
1. Obesity—Psychological aspects.   2. Rational-emotive
psychotherapy.   3. Reducing.   I. Trimpey, Jack.   II. Title.
RC552.025T75   1995
616.85′26—dc20   94-7943 CIP

Manufactured in the United States of America
Published simultaneously in Canada

January 1995

10   9   8   7   6   5   4   3   2   1

BVG

CONTENTS

FOREWORD

The First Book

This, we believe, is a unique book. It is written as a self-help book for people with eating disorders, particularly overeaters, yet it contains no information on what or how much food to eat. You will find no nutritional advice or charts about calories, fat, or cholesterol content, and nowhere inside will you find speculations about the mysteries of human food digestion and metabolism. In these pages, however, you will find a plan for weight control that is revolutionary in its simplicity and clarity. You will also learn a simple mental exercise, Addictive Voice Recognition Technique[sm] (AVRT[sm]), that can tip the scales of weight control in your favor.

Taming the Feast Beast directs dieters toward new attitudes about weight control so the reader can confidently move ahead with the very important business of losing weight. *Taming the Feast Beast* could be considered the lengthy introduction or first long chapter to any good diet book, for its principles provide the psychological basis for successful weight control. *Taming the Feast Beast* could also be billed as the companion volume for *any* diet book, recognizing that there are many excellent eating guides that present lists of foods, helpful hints in preparation, nutritional concepts and information, and menus to follow.

But in reality, this book is the *first* book that should be read by persons who have a serious weight problem and are serious about doing something decisive about it. *Taming the Feast Beast* is not a diet book but instead a general strategy for weight control for people who tend to put on weight and have trouble losing it and keeping it off. When you learn all you want to know about calories, food combinations, recipes, food preparation techniques, fitness, metabolism, genetics, vitamins, fasting, and fadding, then you are ready for Rational Recovery® from fatness. You may also not even use a diet book, if you so choose, because Rational Recovery from fatness is a comprehensive program that is sufficient for achieving moderation and a healthy balance in one's diet. *Taming the Feast Beast* contains no medical or dietary information, and persons who suspect underlying physical causes for obesity or other metabolic problems are urged to seek the counsel of an M.D.

This book makes a convincing argument for weight control through self-control. It is written for people who are skeptical of traditional approaches, including Overeaters Anonymous, diet centers, and many supervised weight reduction programs, and it offers a fresh start for anyone who has tried everything in a quest for weight control but still is unable to achieve and maintain a desired weight. In *Taming the Feast Beast,* the central concept of Rational Recovery has been applied to overeating—Addictive Voice Recognition Technique (AVRT). This simple device is revolutionizing addiction care because of its simplicity, its potency, and its ability to be quickly learned and easily understood. Rational Recovery is not a sugar-coated pill. What you will read here is direct and decisive; you will be moved to act instead of contemplate.

It is your responsibility to educate yourself on your own dietary needs; you have an incredibly large number of books available to draw upon at bookstores and libraries, and your family physician will gladly provide you with specialized information based on his or her knowledge of your body, or you may visit a nutritionist.

Taming the Feast Beast draws upon the rational-emotive behavior therapy (REBT) of Albert Ellis, Ph.D., president, Institute for Rational-Emotive Therapy. Because much in this volume is derived from the seminal works of Dr. Ellis, individual references to Dr. Ellis's works are omitted.

Rational Recovery from Fatness (RR-Fatness) groups are form-ing around the country. The Rational Recovery Self-Help Net-work (RRSN) is devoted to implementing a worldwide network of scientifically based self-help groups. When you have read this book, you may be interested in participating in an RR-Fatness group if there is one in your community. Rational Recovery is now responding to a desperate need in America and elsewhere for a network of self-help groups that are based on self-reliance, reason-ing, and scientific thought rather than on religious/spiritual teach-ings and ideas of dependency on others. If there is no RRS activity in your community, feel free to contact us directly (916-621-2667) and we will provide direct assistance to you in starting a local RR-Fatness project.

Lois Trimpey, M.Ed.
Jack Trimpey, L.C.S.W.

TAMING THE FEAST BEAST

CHAPTER 1

To the Fat One

Whatever Your Present Weight, You Can Lose Pounds Permanently If You Want To

Already, as you read the sentence above, you may notice feelings about your body, about the idea of becoming slimmer, and some uneasy feelings about "dieting." The chances are that because you are reading this book on weight control, you have also read other books—perhaps many books—on the subject, and are still struggling with the old problem. And you may read on, excited at the possibility of getting some new dietary plan, some new understanding of physiology and metabolism, or some new motivational gimmick. There is a natural human tendency for all of us to want solutions to our problems that are simple, quick, and easy. It would be nice if you could set a weight goal for yourself; have a handy set of instructions, including a menu of tasty foods; stick to that plan for a few weeks without undue effort; and then look at yourself in the mirror one day and find a new, slim, and trim you beaming at you, just as in the TV ads that promote such fantasies.

Instead of quick fixes for weight loss, you will find here a viewpoint that you have probably suspected all along: When it comes to losing weight and maintaining that weight, *there is no free lunch.* While some people may veer into a dietary plan that is easy and effective for them, most people will do much better by accepting that it takes *effort* to get slim and trim, and to accept that it takes sustained *discipline* to stay that way.

Sounds grim, doesn't it? And you've been through lots of difficult times, wanting very much, even desperately, to lose weight. You may have suffered through the inconvenience of special food preparation, the cravings, the cheating, the guilt, the hard-won loss of pounds, and then the gradual fattening up again. It gets to look pretty hopeless after a few of these cycles, and it can start to look hopeless that permanent weight loss is even possible.

"But isn't there *some* way for me really to make it happen?" you may be wondering.

To this, the answer is a resounding "Yes." Rational Recovery® (RR) is an approach that helps people like you to adopt *attitudes* that make weight loss and weight control a reality. RR also presents some new insights that can put you in control of your feelings, your behavior, and ultimately your physical dimensions. Although the goals of self-improvement and weight loss are not easy, RR can make them easier, and certainly more attainable than they may have seemed before.

Invasion of the Body-Haters

Being captive in a body you hate is no fun. I (L.T.) know what it is like, because I suffered from fatness for many years. Now that I have made friends with my body (me), I feel much better and I am having more fun. It is also easier for me to maintain a steady weight that is right for me, and I don't feel cheated every time I sit down to eat. The purpose of *Taming the Feast Beast* is to help you also to get along better with your body, to become a more independent person, to lose the weight that you want to lose, and—very importantly—to have more fun.

I have tried more diet approaches than I can remember, and my bookshelf is still filled with many excellent diet books written by intelligent authors giving sound dietary advice. I recommend any and all of them to fat people who want to lose weight.

But none of them answered a very important question, one I

was unable to answer because I didn't know to ask it. This question sets the stage for all that follows, and probably influences the outcome of weight loss efforts more than anything else.

Why Do I Want to Lose Weight in the First Place?

Practically everyone who wants to lose weight would answer, "So I can feel better." So be it. That is a fine motivation to do anything.

But what are the finer dimensions of "feeling better"? For example, while I was fat, I was unaware that I was participating in the great American tradition of people hating their own bodies—disliking themselves. I really thought that my problem was being thirty to forty pounds overweight and that some inner weakness was the cause of my overweight. I struggled year after year with various diets, all of which helped me temporarily to lose some but not all of the weight I intended to lose. When I "finished a diet," I certainly felt better! I was glad to feel lighter on my feet, pleased to look better in tailored clothes, happy when someone complimented me on my looks, felt sexy when my husband's hand caressed my abdomen, appreciative to feel more energized, and very glad to have access to tasty foods in larger quantities. So I would have "a honeymoon," hoping against hope that none of the dreaded pounds would reappear on the scale and that none of the loathsome rolls would again curl over my belt. Invariably, however, I would start cheating on food, and the weight would slowly accumulate, and I would gradually get that sinking feeling of knowing that I had once again lost a huge struggle against myself. The next round of the fight, I could see, would be even more difficult than the one I had just completed successfully and then blown. Periods of guilt and depression became more frequent, and when I would look at myself in the mirror, I would see one who would never achieve real happiness because of some subtle inner defect that kept bringing me down from my temporary and unjustified feelings of satisfaction. But there was always one pleasure that was mine, the dependable friend that could take the edge off the inexplicable empty feeling that seemed a part of my being: tasty food. I could replace worries and other dreary thoughts with ideas of eating, ideas of tasting, chewing, and swallowing, and ideas of nourishment and satiation. I would eat, at odd times of the day, in "extra" amounts, and always the kinds of food that contained the most "flavor punch."

Clearly, I lost weight to gain the advantages of being slimmer, but it is obvious that by "dieting" I was also trying to prove the unprovable and do the undoable. I was trying to prove to myself that I was a worthwhile person, and I was trying to create another "me" that others would admire and that I could accept. That strategy worked temporarily, but then I would become another statistic that proves that overeating is an incurable disease. But, very fortunately, I was able to start questioning myself, as you will learn to do in this book, and get down to the basics of weight control and a happier life. The next question I asked myself was:

Is My Problem Overweight or Fatness?

Terminology is extremely important in solving any problem. Words are powerful symbols, and they determine our beliefs about reality, our emotions, our behavior, and the way we feel about ourselves. In RR you will be using certain words in a special, *exact* way. If asked, "What is your main problem?" you may say it is "overweight," or "overeating," or "compulsive overeating," or "obesity." But these are not really descriptions of your problem. They are only results of it.

In Rational Recovery, all of the above descriptions of your problem are incomplete and inaccurate. Although you may very well be overweight, eat too much, and find it difficult or impossible to control your eating behavior, those facts do not describe your central problem, nor do they suggest any way by which you may solve the problem. The terms "overweight," "overeating," and "obesity" only describe *symptoms* of a condition that is set forth here as "fatness," or *practicing a philosophy that causes emotional distress over one's body and perpetuates the symptoms of overweight, compulsive overeating, obesity, and the weight gain relapse cycle.* You will recognize fatness as a *feeling* you have about your overweight, your overeating, your body, and food itself.

Framing the Problem Correctly

Fatness, while not a disease in itself, is a prevalent condition that can result in severe emotional disturbance among those who are inclined to gain weight. The resulting disturbance makes dietary discipline virtually impossible. Those suffering from fatness also tend to experience serious problems in their social, sexual, and familial roles. Rational Recovery from fatness is a process of learning to think rationally about yourself, about your body, about cravings and appetites, and about some broader issues in life.

I mentioned earlier that for many years I followed the tradition of body-hating. If you are reading here for self-help, then it is quite likely that you, too, have been a victim of social propaganda aimed at getting you to hate your body. It is no secret that our society, and other societies as well, idealize women with thin waists; unblemished complexions; generous, well-formed breasts; and long, slender legs—all in perfect proportion. There may be some biological basis for some versions of sexual beauty, but our culture goes much farther than idealizing the *Playboy* image of feminine (and masculine) beauty. We collectively accept that body image is a criterion for self-acceptance! This disturbing concept that "To accept myself I must have certain physical characteristics," can be seen daily in not-so-subtle messages not only in the media but also in countless examples when individuals such as you and I feel shame for the physical beings we are.

The problem of self-hate is much broader than just concerning fatness, obesity, and overweight. We are a society of self-raters who live by a doctrine of variable human worth and a set of nonsensical rules for attaining self-worth. None of these rules, which are listed a few pages ahead as "Central Ideas of the Philosophy of Fatness," works in your personal interest, and they all contribute in varying degrees to your long-standing difficulty with overeating and overweight.

For you to overcome fatness and then perhaps choose to lose some weight, you must give up some ideas that may turn out to seem even more important to you than food. These are cherished ideas that you may have learned in childhood, possibly from someone you loved and who loved you very much. These ideas seem to be "good, true, and beautiful," yet they spawn the seeds of misery and self-defeat. They are common irrational ideas that cause and perpetuate human unhappiness and result in disturbed relationships. If they could be summed up in a word, it would be *dependence.* Dependence in adults is like perpetual childhood, yet dependence among adults is idealized as good, true, and beautiful. In Rational Recovery, you will learn to become independent wherever that is feasible, and less dependent in other areas—all within a relatively short period and without outside help. After all, getting outside help would be cheating, wouldn't it? We jest, for you may certainly benefit from many kinds of outside help, including psychotherapy, marriage or family counseling, sex therapy, physical therapy, residential treatment, medication, exercise programs, and other related services. But still, we hope you will accept the challenge of weight loss through dietary discipline contained in *Taming the Feast Beast* and not rely excessively on approaches unrelated to your own perseverance and self-determination.

Overeaters in twelve-step programs, for example, are induced to describe themselves as "powerless" in the face of the desire to eat too much and then to surrender their critical judgment to authoritative teachings presented as "suggestions." This works fine for some, but many people cannot accept twelve-step programs. Ads for commercial weight loss programs announce "The XYZ program tells me how to lose weight." This, also, is fine for people who want to rely on personal guidance, weigh-ins, structured eating sessions, and so forth. But most people remain troubled with overweight even though these fine programs exist. For example, consider Harold, whose story follows.

HAROLD

I actually had special shock absorbers installed in my car because it tilted to the driver's side when I drove down the street. I didn't make the change in my car's suspension for any safety reason. It was just because my tilting car attracted too much attention in traffic. People would stare, often smiling at the big man in the poor little car.

One day I saw a sign saying "Weight Loss Center," so I parked my car and walked in. Before long, I weighed in and began a program involving several weight loss centers that cost me thousands of dollars and produced no results. I attended classes, read literature, and talked with their counselors. It all made sense and sounded very easy—eat less, exercise, make a diet plan, and make it work. They even made decisions for me on what and how much to eat. I would go in periodically to weigh in and pick up a week's supply of prepackaged food, just so much per day. When I complained that the weight wasn't coming off as fast as I thought it should, they asked me a lot of questions about what else I was eating in addition to their diet plan food. I felt like an idiot, and they could tell I did, so they said I could see one of their counselors in a few days. I wasn't really interested in counseling, but I went to see the counselor anyhow. She was nice and we talked most of the session about my not wanting to be in counseling. She said it is normal to go through the feelings and disappointments I was experiencing, and then she remarked how important it must be for me to lose weight. The longer I sat there the madder I got, because the more we talked about losing weight the stupider I felt. So I quit that program and decided that I would lose weight for free—all on my own. Fat chance; I never lost an ounce, and in about a month I started up at another center. And then, a few months later, another. I would lose up to about twenty pounds, and then I would gain it all back.

For people like Harold, RR provides a fresh approach, complete with new terms and a new definition of the problem. In RR, "fatness" is regarded as a personal philosophy that is practiced by people who eat more than is good for them. In RR, you will no longer struggle to control your appetite-driven behavior, but instead you may learn a new way of thinking about yourself that allows you to take control of eating behavior that has seemed uncontrollable. In contrast to Harold, read the following material about Charlene, a forty-year-old married career woman who has gained some very important insights about dietary discipline during her participation in an RR group.

Irrational belief 1: If I eat something, I'll feel better.

Most of the time when I don't feel well it is due to my poor eating habits. When I skip a meal, overindulge, or eat foods that are greasy, fatty, or too cold, then I don't feel well, and these conditions lead to the irrational thought that eating something will make me feel better. However, it just doesn't work because I use it as an excuse to overeat. When I am feeling weak or tired and I start eating, generally I will overeat because eating doesn't work, so I keep eating. I don't feel better! Then I get myself in more trouble because I just know that the next thing I eat will be the key. This is totally nuts! I can overcome this irrational habit by adopting sound eating patterns and by allowing myself to relax and enjoy food on a regular schedule. Make meals a high priority. The point to all this meandering is that my irrational belief that food will make me feel better actually backfires on me, and my irrational actions lead me to feel worse! It is time for me to purge this nutty notion.

Irrational belief 2: Food is strength-giving.

Food doesn't give me emotional strength. Food fuels my body, but it does not fortify me against the emotional rigors of daily living. I can't wear my fat as a shield against adversity. Food is ineffective as a barrier to suffering. Actually, overindulgence saps my strength because it takes a lot of energy to digest the extra food I don't need and to carry around excess weight.

Irrational belief 3: Food is my greatest comforter.

How nutty! This is an irrational assignment for the role of food in my life. From a rational standpoint, once my basic needs for nutrition are met, food cannot provide comfort. Food as the great comforter may work on a short-term basis, but in the long run it will exact a high cost. It just isn't appropriate for me to use food as a comforter. Food has served as a poor substitute for the other comforts of life I have denied myself.

Irrational belief 4: Food is my greatest source of satisfaction.

On one of the tests I was administered to determine the level of my well-being I was asked, "Do you feel satisfied?" I had no idea what the question meant because I couldn't place the question in an emotional context. For me, the only time I felt satisfied was when I had overeaten until I was in a stupor. This physical sensation was the only gauge I had for measuring satisfaction. Again, this is an inappropriate role for food. Feeding my body properly will lead to physical satisfaction, but this in no way relates to my emotional satisfaction.

Irrational belief 5: There's nothing I can do about my compulsion to overeat, so there's no use in my trying.

Quit whining! This statement is not only irrational, it is also irritating. First of all, I don't have a compulsion to overeat. I have strongly ingrained habits of overeating, but I'm not compulsive. Habits can be changed; it takes work, but work leads to growth and change, and how satisfying the change will be! Of course I can change. Think about how much I've changed my outlook in the past two or three months. If I can change my attitudes, then I can certainly change my habits.

Additionally, this irrational belief points out the hopelessness I've assigned to a habit. Culturally we espouse the idea that once you fall into a behavior pattern, you are helpless to change the pattern. For example, we make myriad excuses for people who perform criminal acts. We say that they rob and steal and rape and plunder because they come from underprivileged backgrounds or because their mothers didn't love them or because their schools failed them. These may be contributing factors to lead to certain behavior patterns, but they are not reasons! Our behavior is within our command, and when we fall into destructive habits, it is because we have chosen to do so. I can change. I am not helpless.

Irrational belief 6: My poor eating habits are lifelong and can't be altered.

Maybe my habits are lifelong, but they sure can be changed. I am on the way to changing them. Lurking in the back of my mind are all the stories I've heard about how difficult it is for people to maintain their weight loss through dieting. That's why I'm not dieting. I haven't been able to "diet" in the past because I viewed my diets as unpleasantnesses to be endured until I reached a certain weight. Now I'm working on changing my habits, which are the real source of my eating difficulties. Habits can be changed! The secret to changing habits is to replace a bad habit with a good one.

Irrational belief 7: I'm a "good" person when I'm thin and controlling my appetite. I'm "bad" when I overeat, so when I'm feeling negative I overeat to confirm my negative opinion of myself: "See what a bad person I am—just look at how much I've eaten."

There is nothing defensible in this statement. I can't measure myself; I can only measure my behavior. My poor behavior doesn't make me a "bad" person, and my good behavior doesn't make me a "good" person. I am just a living, functioning human being. I can change my behavior. I can think rationally or I can suffer from irrationality if I choose to do so, but no matter what, I can't change my humanity. I can measure my behavior, but I will leave myself alone. There is no need for me to assign an irrational notion of goodness or badness to myself.

Irrational belief 8: If I could control my appetite and control my weight, what else could I go on to control that may be

my heart's desire? What kind of changes would take place? Could I handle the changes, and would they be desirable?

This is an irrational line of questioning. When I say "if I could control my appetite and control my weight," there's a hidden irrationality. It is not a matter of "if I could" but "if I choose to" or "if I want to control my appetite."

Just changing my eating habits will be just a change in my habits, nothing more and nothing less. There is no magic imbued inside me that will be released when I become thinner. I'll be the same self, but I'll have better habits.

I may have preoccupied myself with eating to forestall changes in other facets of my life. If indeed I have been doing that, then this preoccupation is just another good reason for me to alter my habits to rid myself of this irrational approach. Changing my eating habits doesn't mean that I will have to change my life.

Irrational belief 9: Overeating is the only way to deal with my frustrations.

Overeating may be the only way I have chosen to deal with my frustrations, but it is certainly not the only avenue open to me. I can take a walk, go swimming, or if possible, I can work to change the frustration.

Irrational belief 10: I can't enjoy a meal just for the pleasure of the act of eating and the taste and texture of the food I'm consuming. I must overeat to get pleasure from eating.

This is really nutty. I have chosen not to allow myself to enjoy food because I thought I wasn't entitled to enjoyment, and if I enjoyed food, then I might start enjoying other things in my life and unworthy people shouldn't enjoy anything. Of course I can enjoy food in moderation. The notion of worthy or unworthiness is irrational, and it is inappropriate when I apply it to myself.

Food is one of life's pleasures. I can enjoy food appropriately. I can enjoy each morsel and savor the taste, texture, fragrance, and appear-

ance of my food. How much better this approach is than the irrational approach I've taken of overloading my body. I've perverted my enjoyment, but my body has found a way to have its pleasure.

Irrational belief 11: Fun is exclusively the province of undesirable food. In other words, I can derive pleasure only from sugary, fatty, and snack-type foods.

The irrationality of this statement gets back to the measuring stick I've applied to myself. I've felt that some foods are bad and some are good. Food may be put to good or bad use, but food is just like people: It just is, it isn't good or bad. It may not be good for my body, but by ingesting the "bad" food I am not making myself a "bad" person. I may make myself sick, but I am not making myself bad. Food is not an appropriate vehicle for expressing a rebellious nature.

Irrational belief 12: I shouldn't get nervous or tense.

Here is a "should" that I will purge. I get nervous or tense because of my thought processes. I am learning to change my thoughts, so I am not as tense or as nervous as I was. I would prefer that I not get tense or nervous, but if I do, I can approach the situation from a rational standpoint and examine my feelings to ferret out the irrationalities so I can rid myself of the tension.

Irrational belief 13: I can't stand anxiety.

I may not like anxiety, but I can stand it. After all, I'm still alive, and I've created enough anxiety for myself that if anxiety led to quick death, I would have been gone a long time ago.

Irrational belief 14: I can't stand being frustrated, so I turn to food for calming.

Well, I can stand being frustrated. I may not like it, but I can stand it. There are times in everyone's life when frustration is unavoidable. Enduring frustration (if the situation cannot be changed) will lead to greater strength of character. Turning to food is not an appropriate solution because it is physically harmful, and in the long term it leads to additional frustration.

Irrational belief 15: If something goes wrong, it has to be my fault, and I can't stand failure.

There's no way that everything that goes wrong in my life is my fault. Something may go wrong because of an action I have taken or a decision I have made, but the only way to keep that from happening would be for me to quit living, and that's not an alternative I'm interested in. In addition, there's another irrationality. I am assuming that I have complete control over more of my life than I do. Many factors are beyond my control. As far as failure is concerned, I can stand failure. Again, I may not like it, but I can stand it. Some of the most worthy lessons in my life have resulted from my most abysmal failures. To give up these lessons and learning experiences I would have to give up failing, and I'd rather continue to grow and learn. Failure never occurs without action, and I want to continue to act.

Irrational belief 16: Do I really want to lose weight?

No, weight loss is not my goal. Healthy eating habits and improving my diet are my real goals. Of course, I'll lose weight as a matter of course, but if I don't, it won't be the end of the world. Yes, I do want to give up my inappropriate insulation. But changing my eating habits will be just a change in habits—nothing more and nothing less. It certainly won't be reflected in my image of myself. I am giving up grading and measuring my self-worth by my weight. I am giving up the notion of self-worth.

Irrational belief 17: I can't bear self-denial.

Evidently I can bear it because I've been using it as a strategy to forestall dealing with my poor eating habits. By eating too much, I've denied myself the healthy body I've wanted. By eating properly, I will be allowing myself something I want very much, not denying myself *something. A little momentary self-denial will result in a long-term gain of health.* *

By reading further, you may learn to think in a way that allows you to eat correctly on a permanent basis. When you first begin to eat correctly, your appetite will undergo some changes, and finally, when you have achieved a desirable weight for a period of time, you are "rationally recovered" from overeating. Then it is time to kick the recovery habit and *get a life,* free of nagging fear of relapse, with eating correctly as second nature, and without undue concern about past problems.

Remember that you will not achieve personal perfection in RR. If you should achieve perfection, the authors hereby warn you that some people in the Vatican will surely find out about this. You will, of course, be made eligible for sainthood, and a shelf—high in a far-off cathedral—will be dusted off in preparation for a statue of you. A representative from the Vatican, possibly a bishop or a cardinal, will pay a visit to your home and you will eventually become "Saint [your name]." Surely that is not your goal in losing weight. Or is it?

The Help Menu

Americans are troubled about the results of eating incorrectly, and they are also troubled about the behavior of eating itself. Americans are misinformed and seduced into beliefs about eating and dietary plans that are unhelpful, unrealistic, frustrating, counterproductive, and very often downright unhealthy.

We are provided large amounts of delicious, unhealthy food to eat, and then informed that overeating is a *disease.* Each month a new report is issued by some research or health organization proclaiming a new slant on nutrition, and the latest advice from peo-

* Reprinted from *The Journal of Rational-Emotive & Cognitive-Behavior Therapy,* Vol. 8, No. 4 (Winter 1990), with permission of Human Sciences Press, Inc.

ple in white lab coats usually conflicts with last year's advice from people with stethoscopes hanging from their necks. Food containing iron, always regarded as wholesome and good for one's energy level, is now identified as a cause of heart disease. Margarine, once preferred over butter to prevent artery disease, is now found to be equally as "bad." Chocolate, once regarded as bad for heart and teeth, is now presented as "good cholesterol" and an antidecay agent. Oat bran, hyped for an entire year as preventing or even reversing heart disease, is now presented in the media as not substantially different from any other source of fiber in the diet.

Through the mass media, Americans are becoming conditioned to follow the bouncing ball to live their lives. Whatever is dangled before them on the tube becomes the latest fad, the most urgent health mandate, the most "advanced concept," or the most stunning breakthrough in healthful living.

New books appear regularly describing how what you eat is critically important. For example, it is said lately that fat is the culprit in overweight—that is, if you don't eat fat, you won't get fat. While for many this may be quite true, adhering to a low-fat diet may be quite inconvenient, frustrating, unsatisfying, and even ineffective for others. Vegetarian, low-cholesterol diets are conducive to weight loss, but that does not mean that anyone *should* become a vegetarian.

A wave of media reporting is now challenging the idea of dietary discipline. A story in *The Washington Post* on April 2, 1992, reports that no matter what approach people use, virtually nothing succeeds in helping them keep weight off. A review of industry-supplied data found that programs such as Jenny Craig, Weight Watchers, and Nutri-System, and commercial diet aids such as Ultra Slimfast and other diet preparations and drugs have dropout rates of about 80 percent. While these programs may help many to lose up to 10 percent of their body weight in the short term, virtually all of them fail over the long term. Usually two thirds of the weight is regained within one year, and virtually all of it within five years. The article concludes with this interesting comment from researchers at the National Institutes of Health: "For most overweight persons, the condition is a lifelong challenge."

Yes—there is the "C" word again: *challenge*. But look at what is happening in our culture. An exciting new "antidiet" movement was described in a subsequent *Newsweek* article, "Let Them Eat Cake" (August 17, 1992). The article included a picture of two women rejoicing before an open refrigerator, one of them eating some ice cream. We learn from this media source that the National Institutes of Health conference "gave the kiss of death on dieting's face" when it pointed out the ineffectiveness of weight loss programs and products. The challenge of dietary discipline was nowhere mentioned, and "yo-yo dieting" was presented as worse than staying fat. The article asserts that weight control is mainly a medical remedy for chronic health conditions and suggests that overweight people learn to accept that it is okay to be fat. The article then introduces a group sponsored by psychologists in New York, Overcoming Overeating (OO), which encourages people to eat everything they want. Group members are seen in another picture eating cookies and other concentrated sweets during a meeting. Their expectation is that the human body is self-correcting, so that when they are satiated for a period of time (placating the inner child?), they will somehow come to crave broccoli as much as chocolate. So effortless. So perfect. So fully packed they will be. But will they lose weight? Some undoubtedly will, and others certainly won't, as one participant affirms. "The program feels so good and so right," she says, "but deep inside there's a lower weight I'd prefer. I feel comfortable where I am, and I can stay here if this is where I'm meant to stay."

Stay the Course

Do we really need legions of scientists to map out matters of personal health and hygiene for us? It may be interesting that the high-fat diet of Eskimos and other wilderness dwellers doesn't result in high rates of heart disease, that many who smoke a lot do live to advanced ages, and that sheepherders of tribes in the Himalayas live longer than Scandinavians who don't exercise regularly. But your life in your community is uniquely your own, and you will ultimately decide what is appropriate for you to eat, whether to smoke or to drink alcohol, how much to exercise, and what to do for work and pleasure.

A common promise of diet books is that diets grow easy with time. They don't. Many sincere readers of these books find that they do not get the promised relief from hunger and craving after many weeks of discipline, and they give up in exasperation. Other diet experts promise that one may eat whatever one wants, or as much as one wants, and still maintain a desired weight. These plans should be investigated and considered, but it should not be surprising to find that if something sounds too good to be true, it probably is. To the contrary of many packaged programs and expert opinions, the "correct eating" described herein includes whatever one sensibly chooses to eat—but, *of course,* in moderate amounts. Correct eating, as you will see in a later chapter, is not a diet at all, but rather a life-style you can enter.

What's Rational?

"Rational," a vital term throughout *Taming the Feast Beast,* refers to the quality of one's thinking at any given moment, not in a good-bad context, but in respect to the following parameters, as set forth by rational-emotive behavior therapist and theoretician Maxie Maultsby, M.D.:

1. Does my thinking in this situation help me to remain healthy and alive?
2. Is what I'm thinking *objectively true,* or am I being judgmental? Is there evidence to support this opinion or belief? Am I using words according to their real meaning?
3. Does my thinking in this situation lead to feelings I want to have?
4. Does my thinking help me to reach a goal I have chosen?
5. Does my thinking minimize conflict with others?

These five criteria are listed in approximate order of significance, and any line of thought can be evaluated against these questions. An idea can fail on one or two criteria and still be fairly rational, because rational thought is self-forgiving, or nonperfectionistic.

It all boils down to a style of thinking that gets you what you want, keeps you out of trouble, makes you feel good, and helps you cope with unpleasant realities. The catch, however, is that rational lines of thought are *objectively* true. This means that in RR, we challenge many beliefs that *seem* to be obviously true, and learn that there is no evidence or proof to support them. When we see that a belief is false, we are then left with a conclusion that is "rational."

For example, you may hear someone who is depressed about being overweight say, "I must lose weight." On the surface, this may sound like a reasonable statement, but only until the questioning, or disputing, begins. "Why *must* you lose weight?" is a good question, and in asking this we find no reason whatsoever. If one tries to support the irrational "must" by speaking of advantages ("I will feel better"), the next question is, naturally, "Why must you feel better?" If one speaks of disadvantages ("Because my clothes don't fit") of being overweight, then the next question is, naturally, "Why *must* your clothes fit?" Finally, with some mental effort, perhaps, it will occur to most people that "It is *unnecessary* for me to lose weight, but I *want* to lose weight." In Rational Recovery, we avoid what psychologist Albert Ellis, Ph.D., calls "musturbation" as a matter of principle and reason. "Must" is a rotten word that sabotages dietary discipline.

As you can see, both rational and irrational thinking in the form of self-talk is something that all of us practice daily in our lives, at least to some extent. We *naturally* want our beliefs to be true; we want to survive; we prefer positive moods over negative ones, pleasure over pain; and so on. The difficulty is that as human beings we are naturally and biologically prone to sloppy and crooked thinking, to gullibility, to magical and superstitious thinking, to short-term pleasures instead of long-term happiness, and especially to accept negative evaluations of our intrinsic worth and then think poorly of ourselves and experience feelings of unworthiness.

These tendencies comprise the Achilles' heel of overweight persons, whose inherent fallibilities are magnified by the presence of fat, a highly visible symbol of one's inadequacy, unworthiness, and inferiority.

In Rational Recovery, we have a comprehensive system of self-help wherein the overweight person can quickly come to terms with the central issues of fatness and of recovery. Drawing heavily from the rational-emotive behavior therapy of Albert Ellis, RR identifies several specific irrational ideas and beliefs that perpetuate the compulsive life-styles of fat people, and then provides the means to change one's own emotions and behavior. The resulting improvement in one's functioning may be regarded as basic personality change.

As you read in the following section about the philosophy of fatness, you will probably notice a peculiar feeling of emotional lightness. This is caused by the introduction of rational thoughts into your current thinking. Take note of this feeling if it occurs, as it is scientific evidence showing that *you feel the way you think* and that you therefore have far more control over your emotions and behavior than you ever dreamed possible. What you are about to read will not cause any shift in mood or feeling, but the changes you notice are caused directly by *your own thoughts*. You can accentuate the "rational high" by shifting back and forth between the irrational (italicized) and rational phrases in each numbered idea. Enjoy yourself as you read.

Central Ideas of the Philosophy of Fatness

1. I am powerless over my urges to eat food and therefore not in control of, or responsible for, what I put into my mouth,
instead of the rational idea that I have considerable voluntary control over my extremities and facial muscles.

2. To feel like a worthwhile person, I must have a "presentable" appearance that no one will find unappealing, unattractive, ugly, fat, overweight, homely, or even plain,

instead of the rational idea that while there are clearly some advantages to looking good to others, I am not dependent on the approval or admiration of others for my sense of personal worth.

3. To build self-esteem or respect myself, I must lose weight,
   instead of the rational idea that it is *because* I accept and respect myself that I will limit the food I ingest.

4. My painful emotions and cravings for food are often intolerable and therefore must be controlled by eating food,
   instead of the rational idea that some discomfort is a necessary, inevitable, and entirely harmless part of losing weight.

5. It is a dire necessity for adults to be loved, accepted, and approved of,
   instead of the rational idea that adults do not have to get what they want, including love, respect, and acceptance. Rejection is just another's opinion of my worth, one with which I may gullibly agree or rationally disagree. I choose to accept or love myself simply because it feels better than to dislike myself. In this matter, mine is the final word.

6. Because I have committed certain acts, or behaved offensively, or harmed someone, I should moralistically blame and condemn myself,
   instead of the rational idea that as a human being I am uniquely fallible. I may feel regret, remorse, or sadness for my behavior and mistakes, but I need not conclude that I am a worthless person.

7. Because I am overweight from eating too much, I should moralistically blame and condemn myself,
   instead of the rational idea that people of all weights may enjoy unconditional self-worth, provided they are willing to assert that worth strongly.

8. To consider myself a worthwhile person, I must be competent, intelligent, talented, and achieving in all possible respects, and to fail in any significant way, such as by putting weight back on, is to prove what I've always suspected and feared—that I am a defective, inferior, and worthless person who can never achieve real happiness in life,

instead of the rational idea that doing is more important than doing well, trying is the first step toward succeeding, and accepting myself *now* as a fallible yet inestimably worthwhile human being is entirely possible.

9. If "things" aren't the way I want them very much to be, then it's terrible, horrible, awful, and catastrophic,

instead of the rational idea that "terrible" and "awful" are magical words meaning "worse than most unfortunate." Since nothing can be more than 100 percent bad, I can learn to *accept* life's most serious disappointments, even death. "Things," therefore, don't have to be any particular way for me to be relatively calm and reasonably happy most of the time. It is far better to focus on how to change or control adverse conditions than to "catastrophize" or "awfulize" about them.

10. It is easier to avoid than to face directly certain self-responsibilities, such as reducing the amount of food I ingest and concentrating on personal growth,

instead of the rational idea that the "easy way," especially continuing to overeat, is invariably much harder and more painful in the long run.

11. Because I've lost a few pounds, I absolutely must not gain them back, no matter what, because then I will be defeated and the struggle will become hopeless,

instead of the rational idea that as time in Rational Recovery goes by, overeating comes to appear increasingly stupid because of the obvious selfish advantages of correct eating. When I do occasionally overeat, however, it won't be awful or terrible because I will then resume prudence—selfishly, guiltlessly, and very quickly.

12. Because I am substantially overweight from overeating, I need something or someone stronger or greater than myself upon which to rely,
instead of the rational idea that dependency is my original problem, and it is better to start now to take the risks of thinking and acting independently.

13. Because fatness (the preoccupation with food, body weight, and appearance) once greatly affected my life, it will continue to affect me frequently and indefinitely,
instead of the rational idea that self-acceptance and correct eating are self-fulfilling. Because there is so much more to life than a constant struggle to lose weight, I can gradually refocus my attention and become vitally absorbed in activities and projects outside of myself that are unrelated to food and my physical dimensions.

14. The reasons for my overweight condition are buried in my past and in my immensely fascinating and complex psyche. I am overeating for reasons that only very intelligent and highly educated persons can understand,
instead of the rational idea that calories are transformed into fat, and my overweight is directly related to the amount of food I ingest per unit of time, minus the energy expended in my daily life. While I may have learned some patterns of self-defeat in the past, my present overweight and emotional disturbances are caused by certain irrationalities in my present personal philosophy.

15. Somewhere out there, there is a perfect antidote to life's problems, and until I find it, I am doomed to a life of uncertainty and turmoil,
instead of the rational idea that uncertainty is the spice of life, and seeking a perfect solution is silly and a waste of time. I will do better to view life as an enjoyable experiment, seeking my own pleasures and my own personal growth.

By reading and rereading the ideas above, you may immediately notice their interconnections. This insight is the rational consciousness that helps one to maintain a desired weight and that provides the basis for continuous personal growth. In a later chapter we will examine each rational concept in a little more detail to establish weight loss as rooted in reason.

However, it is good to view the above core beliefs against the backdrop of cultural values in American society. Overweight people are victims of propaganda that not only affects them personally, as above, but also determines how our health care system attempts to help them. In most communities, there are three systems that offer help to the overweight: (1) fee-for-service weight loss clinics, clubs, and plans; (2) medical care with inpatient and outpatient programs; and (3) support groups. Rational Recovery *self-help* groups are the emerging fourth system that is available to overweight people. By self-help we refer to any group of people who gather around a common problem to overcome that problem, and then leave the group when the problem is solved.

The first three of these systems tend to perpetuate the myth that people with eating disorders are *fundamentally dependent people who "need" outside help*. The first system, entrepreneurial, provides structure, authority in the form of supervision and weigh-ins, and motivation in the form of financial investment, and some even provide the actual food materials to those who are "powerless" to provide those things for themselves.

The second system, medical, provides external solutions to the inner problem in the form of the doctor persona (higher power); drugs; fasting schedules and dieting lists; and cutting of the body, as in fat removal and restructuring of the alimentary canal.

The third system, support groups, is a valuable social resource for people with specialized problems, and because they are based on the tradition of people helping people, they are available anywhere. Take Off Pounds Sensibly and Weight Watchers (although a fee is involved) are good examples of support groups that empower the individual to lose extra pounds. One serious drawback of support groups, however, is that they sometimes tend to foster dependency and quite often stray from the higher purposes of personal growth and self-reliance. Although special groups exist for people with stressful health problems (cancer, stroke, colostomy, blindness, etc.), other support groups exist for people who have suffered great losses or who have unusual personal problems (bereavement and grief, spouses of prisoners, parents of ill children, etc.). These valuable groups, which allow for sharing and learning strategies for coping, provide the comfort of recognition to people who are not regarded as sick or deficient but who feel alone in their personal struggles against adversity. They are generally spontaneous meetings of people with a common problem. There is usually someone who facilitates or leads in discussion, and the group develops its own norms and techniques for problem-solving. People confide their problems, share their sorrows, reach out to others, come and go as they please, and the general tone is "Accentuate the positive."

Dependency Groups

Unfortunately, self-help is a misnomer for what is offered in most communities to those suffering compulsive overeating. Some support groups, especially twelve-step spiritual healing groups, go much further with the idea of support in that they actively teach people that they *need* the support of the group to cope with the common identified problem. Over time, certain philosophies and practices of the group have been formulated into an incontestable creed; newcomers are obliged to "come to believe" as the support group does, even if it takes many years to "work the whole program." Members become confident that their common beliefs comprise the "one true way" to deal with the presenting problem, if not for the enjoyment of life itself. Collectively, members of these groups enjoy a sense of having tapped into a ruling ideology, and believe that all human beings might do well to become dependent on twelve-step groups. These groups would better be called *dependency groups,* because the avenue to the desired goal always involves emotional dependence on the group and on its articles of faith. Newcomers who present specific life problems, such as gambling, drinking, lusting, overeating, or overspending, are often quite surprised and disappointed to find that there is much, much

more to getting better than learning better ways of thinking, acting, and feeling. Invariably the dependency group presumes to
know what is best for the newcomer, even to the point of sug-
gesting that the newcomer might regard the dependency group as
"God." Many who come to these dependency groups are desperate
for anything that will help, so they accept the invitation to turn
their entire lives over to the group in exchange for symptom relief.
For them, relief is at hand, for now there is an entirely new preoccupation in life to supplant the original problem. Within the nurturing confines of the dependency group, life is much safer and
more predictable. Submission, members report, "works."

For the rest of us, submission doesn't work because we are simply unable to submit. We are convinced that we can "see through"
the concepts that make the dependency groups so popular. Try as
we might, we cannot force ourselves to accept their articles of
faith. For us, there is a fourth system that is more consistent with
the *nature* of our problem, the problem of overweight. If dependency is the central issue in fatness, then rational *self-help,* with its
emphasis on personal independence, is very likely the most relevant solution.

CHAPTER 2

If Only I Could Understand Why

So much has been written and said about the reasons for obesity that it is little wonder that we fat people have had a difficult time doing anything about it. Here are some actual examples of "Why I'm overweight" that have been offered in RR discussions.

"I think it started during my adolescence, when I started to want to go out with boys. My mother was against dating, so she started overfeeding me so I'd get fat and ugly and then the boys wouldn't look at me."

"I'm just naturally overweight. My body has slow metabolism. My mother was overweight, too."

"I eat to push down feelings that are coming up. You see, I have this energy coming up—bad energy—and I have to push it down or I get miserable. After I eat, though, I get guilty and miserable anyhow, so I eat more."

"I was molested as a child and so I got fat to prevent any more sexual attention. That didn't work and my father kept molesting me so I kept eating as a way of getting even with my mother, who hated to see me fat but wasn't doing anything to protect me from Dad."

"Every time I try to think about my childhood I get all uptight and end up raiding the refrigerator. I must have been molested, even though I can't remember it, and I'm eating and getting fat to get even with my parents."

"Having a baby changed my body."

"I reward and punish myself with food. Sometimes I eat when I'm guilty as punishment and sometimes I eat too much to reward myself when I've been good."

"If I feel depressed or lonesome, I binge on sweets. It's like a tranquilizer. I feel good at least for a little while, but then I feel rotten later."

"I haven't been using my Higher Power. I'm out of touch with it."

"I control others by eating. They know if I get mad I'll start eating too much. It doesn't work, but that's what I do. Actually, I comfort myself when I don't get my way, when I can't control others."

"For me, hunger is an emotion and I can't handle it except by eating something."

"I'm busy on step 4, and when that is taken care of I'll come down in weight."

"Eating is a substitute for love. It fills me up when I'm emotionally empty."

"I've been so hurt in my personal relations that I now hide in my fat body."

"I haven't been working the program the way I should."

"I'm a codependent and that's what causes me to overeat. I cover up my emotions when my inner child is hurting."

Persons who persist in believing the above statements will probably not be able to solve their eating disorders. These statements do not explain why one is overweight or eating too much; they only describe what a person may be thinking about as he or she downs another omelet. These ideas of past roots of present behavior provide a powerful support for compulsive overeating but offer nothing in the way of personal change. On the contrary, each person above is saying in effect, either "I overeat because of circumstances over which I have no control—past circumstances," or "I overeat because of complex psychological drives that make me a wonderfully interesting person, at least to my current therapist."

One of the most irrational concepts in the field of weight control is the idea that by looking into the past and gaining insight into earlier circumstances, one may find it easier to resist the desire to overeat. For example, a man recently appeared on TV promoting the idea that infants born between 1944 and 1960 are suffering from a posttraumatic stress disorder stemming from scheduled feeding during the first two years of life. Those who were fed on demand, he stated, turned out to be more functional adults. He launched into a criticism of postwar parenting philosophies that supported the practice of allowing infants to "cry it out" when they are restless and irritable. This kind of pointless crying, according to his developmental scheme, is really not so pointless; the crying is for food—specifically sugar—and he described how a mere taste of sugar water will send even the most disturbed infant into dreamland. He described how the inhuman practice of scheduled feeding is unheard of in other cultures. The trauma of low blood sugar, he reasoned, causes emotional wounds that persist into adulthood and that result in *compensatory overeating.* The solution to this unhappy condition, which he said is affecting millions of overweight people, is to get in touch with one's inner child, to regress into an infantlike state, relive the horror of abandonment in the crib, to sense being plunged into an eternity of deprivation that is known only to infants, and to then experience the caring and love that is the only ointment for emotional healing, to savor sugar, preferably fructose, during the regressed state, and then, over a prolonged time of loving one's inner child, eat small amounts of sugar on a prescribed (ritual) schedule, thus allowing the emotional scars to heal. Then—and only then—he explained, could one's ravenous appetite for food attain normal proportions and could one lose weight.

Now, it is certainly true that infants, when unfed or craving sugar, are truly and completely miserable. And it is quite understandable that eating sugar on a prescribed basis, rather than as contained in doughnuts, cakes, and milk shakes, may result in weight loss. But to conclude that the problem of overeating is caused by decades-old frustrations and miseries, and to relive those experiences in guided imagery or hypnosis as a means to refuse a second helping, is a leap of logic that would amaze an alchemist. But when one is unhappily overweight, and has tried many avenues to weight control without success, troubled logic is often more appealing than no hope, and very often more appetizing than dietary discipline. Consequently, the truth about weight loss is lost in a sea of wish fulfillment—the wish that weight loss is a reward for suspending one's own critical judgment.

The messengers of magic are having their day in American health care, speaking of behavior as disease, overeating as addictive disease, overeating as a symptom of something else, and mysterious procedures that produce results. The result for millions of well-fed dieters is dependency in daily living, dependency on anything but one's own free will to restrict food intake.

It is interesting that the terms "dependent" and "passive" have often been linked in psychological literature, and it is no coincidence that here, in the statements above, overweight people are demonstrating a remarkable degree of passivity, and more importantly, dependence. To illustrate passivity in seemingly energetic plans for weight loss, let's look at several typical contemporary approaches.

The example above wherein overeating is described on TV as a compensation for childhood deprivations, may result in a viewer seeking professional help. He or she may attend weekly sessions and cooperate diligently with the "treatment," which may include hypnosis, past-oriented discussions, painful self-disclosure, distressing sessions of "getting it all out," and straining to comprehend the logic of self-awareness. But the goal of getting help is to lose weight, and while the sessions and fees for services pile up, one may continue eating more food than is necessary to maintain one's weight. The promise of therapeutic intervention is a reduction of the desire to eat, plus more ability to refuse extra food. Yet this change is expected to come about magically, with no serious or intense effort to make those specific changes. This is an extremely passive role for the client, even though he or she is investing considerable time, energy, money, and effort in the therapeutic activities. The passivity is toward hunger itself, and the dependency is upon a theory that supported that passivity. The client is quite dependent on the judgment of the therapist, because the theory of addictive disease, as we shall see below, is incoherent. So, as one's commitment to the therapeutic process increases, passivity also increases, and the dependency on the therapist may also become more pronounced. Sadly, weight may also increase, due to the complete lack of effort in the critical area of dietary discipline.

The "specialized diet" approach, in spite of its intensity and discomfort, is also quite passive, and dependent on mysterious means for change. While the dieter, for example, struggles to eat only grapefruit and buttermilk with crumpets, he or she imagines wonderful processes at work inside. The dieter visualizes fat globules dissolving in acetic acid, while calcium races like an arrow to deactivate the hunger centers of the brain, while the carbohydrates give instant energy that is desperately needed to continue the struggle against the self. These, at least, are the kinds of images that many dieters have of what is going on inside their bodies. They may take some extra manganese to prevent fatigue, and some vitamin E to fortify the immune system while nutrition is low. They read and spend extensively seeking the "chemical key" that will make pounds and inches vanish, with little discomfort, little real effort, and as rapidly as possible. When cravings and weaknesses mount, defenses against them weaken, and finally grapefruit becomes only part of breakfast, buttermilk is for pancakes, and crumpets sit on the edge of a plate heaped with tasty food. The passivity has been toward hunger itself, and the dependency was upon a theory that supported that passivity.

Support groups such as Weight Watchers, Take Off Pounds Sensibly, and Overeaters Anonymous are helpful for many people, but even more find them ineffective. By joining a group of similarly troubled people, one may learn practical ideas about dietary discipline and may also benefit from the social experience of the group. But there is an implicit idea that support groups will make it easier to resist hunger and that without the group it will be harder to eat correctly. That's right: The group member's passivity toward hunger is reinforced by the opinions of others in the group who report that it would have been impossible to lose weight without being there. "Gee, I'm glad I'm here. This will make it easier," most newcomers think when they start attending support groups. Each support group has its own theory on how it makes weight loss easier, either through monitoring, celebrations, moral inventories, use of prepackaged portions, special recipes, Higher Powers, or other specialized means. The passivity is toward hunger itself, and the dependency is upon various theories and activities that support that passivity.

Co-what?

A most unfortunate development in recent years for those caught up in dependencies, compulsive disorders, substance abuse, and other patterns of self-defeat is the emergence of the term "codependency." It is difficult to imagine a more antitherapeutic jargon term than one that obscures the actual meaning of the root word, "depend": "to exist by virtue of a necessary condition or relation; to be determined; to place reliance or trust" *(Webster's Seventh New Collegiate Dictionary).* The prefix "co-" adds nothing to the word "dependent," and to label oneself "codependent" is self-stigmatizing and self-limiting.

You can understand codependency literature and the people who speak of it by lopping off the "co-" that was cutely added to "dependency" about a decade ago.

Overeaters often say, "My moods *depend* on what happens to me and what others say and so I *depend* on others for definitions of my human worth. I *depend* on my body to metabolize food rapidly so I can eat 'normally.' My emotions *depend* on what happened during my childhood. I *depend* on food to ease my disturbed emotions. Although I am an adult, I *depend* on my (parents/spouse/therapist/recovery group/guru/expert) to think correctly for me, to make decisions for me, to tell me what's right and wrong with me, and to tell me what to do with my life. I *depend* on others to make me feel lovable, decent, and acceptable to myself—and all this because I cannot think these things for myself. I *depend* on something greater than the inadequate slob I am to give me the strength, wisdom, character, and serenity I will need to start eating correctly and get down to a desirable, steady weight. I *depend* on someone or some scheme to come along that will make weight loss fun, comfortable, tasty, easy, and fascinating, and until that wonderful person or scheme comes along, I am doomed to continuous overeating and overweight. I *depend* on my eventual success in becoming slim and attractive to consider myself a worthwhile person. I *depend* on the universe to take great interest in me and treat me fairly, and therefore I greatly resent the genes that have made me inclined to be heavy."

If you recognize any of these irrational themes in your thinking, you are in a good position to do something about your own philosophy of fatness.

"But," one may ask, "isn't support an important part of personal change? Isn't that why there are so many support groups? Isn't Rational Recovery itself a network of support groups for overeaters?"

Rational Recovery is a *self*-help program in the literal sense of the word. We know that personal change is a self-inspired process, undertaken out of self-interest. Even in psychotherapy with a professional therapist, change occurs only when one becomes his or her own therapist and decides to change some crooked thinking. Rational Recovery Systems, recognizing that living in an irrational society is a serious deterrent to personal growth, provides local RR-Fatness groups as part of the recovery process. In these groups, people get together and discuss rational concepts as they apply to their own lives and to others in the group. Direct feedback from others in the group is extremely useful in discovering our own irrationalities, because it is often difficult to be objective about our own thinking. For many it is easier to retain and practice shared values in a group than by privately reading information from the printed page. However, we also know that personal change can also be a private experience based on new knowledge; were this not so, self-help books would not have such popularity.

Independence is the central message of Rational Recovery, and when one has achieved the goals of self-acceptance and control of one's negative emotions, it is time to leave the group. Weight loss is incidental to the recovery process, and members may choose to lose as much or as little weight as they like using any "diet" or method that makes sense. In the following chapters you will discover exactly how you can achieve these self-determined goals.

Defeating Passivity and Dependency

In Rational Recovery, *emotional independence* is the foundation for control over hunger itself and the moods that lead up to overeating. This is accomplished through intellectual insight—the same mental activity you are exercising as you read this page. When you can finally see that each emotion, feeling, or mood is the direct reflection of some conscious thought, belief, image, or idea, you will suddenly be in direct control of your emotions and resulting behavior.

Living in our irrational society doesn't help in this intellectual quest, though, because it is widely held that there are other, more significant, and more powerful determiners of emotion than our conscious minds. Take note of the rationalizations made by overweight people at the beginning of this chapter that suggest that there is some other mind that resides in the psyche, a subconscious or unconscious mind that has control of our actions and feelings, one that is more subtle and powerful than our puny conscious thoughts, and one that operates against our sincere wishes to do better in life. Also note the remarks that reflect the idea that the past is an all-important determiner of our present feelings and behaviors.

In a rational context, dependence takes several forms. The first and most recognizable form is emotional dependence, such as when people believe that their emotions are somehow forced on them by other people, by circumstances, or by certain events. If, for example, one's mate is rude or uncooperative, one may become angry or depressed by thinking, "I can't stand being treated this way. He/she should know that I can't function without his/her support and cooperation, and he/she should treat me more fairly. He/she is making me feel angry, and this is a depressing situation." Here the unhappy spouse is depending on the other to be or become different than he/she is, and then blaming and condemning that person, not only for acting poorly, but also for directly causing the angry and depressed emotions that ensue. Relief from these disturbed emotions may then be found in the unrelated but nevertheless tranquilizing activity of overeating.

As you read on, you will be challenged to become an activist on your own behalf and to accept the obvious responsibilities that are part of weight control. Don't worry. If you have read this far with sincere interest, you are almost certainly capable of defeating your addiction to food and learning to eat correctly.

Our Nutty Culture

Our culture powerfully reinforces ideas of dependency, especially upon social approval. For example, the expression "peer pressure" is often heard even in professional offices as an explanation of why so-and-so is behaving in an antisocial, self-defeating way. Adolescents, it is commonly and irrationally believed, have an *overwhelming need* for the approval and acceptance of their peers (agemates) to feel like worthwhile beings and to function in the home, school, and community. Because they have this "need," the reasoning goes, they are under great "pressure" from their peers to conform to behaviors, attitudes, and appearances.

Peer pressure? What kind of pressure is it? Where is this pressure? What presses against what? Can some gauge measure it? In pounds? Ounces? Here we have an excellent example of how patterns of underachievement and self-defeat are fostered and perpetuated within our school system. Of course there is no such thing as "peer pressure." Just a little objective thought, however, will show that there is certainly such a thing as *peer dependency,* based on the nutty, institutionalized idea that social approval is a direct determiner of adolescent emotion and behavior. From this error flows an unending stream of schemes to "motivate" adolescents to "be good," to refuse drugs, to earn good grades, and to behave in civil ways. At the same time, the adolescents are grasping at social status by being "bad," by taking drugs, by defaulting academically, and by attending school for the perverse pleasure of subverting adult authority. By catering so diligently to the "psychological needs" of youngsters, we create a youthful cult of contagious mediocrity and prideful underachievement.

Among adults, the same irrational philosophy of psychological need (for love, approval, and acceptance) persists, but now the dependency is dignified in romantic literature, greeting cards, churches that act as brokerages for self-esteem, and even in massive social research projects such as one in California that recently spent five million tax dollars arriving at the irrational conclusions that self-esteem is "a feeling that one is capable of managing life's challenges" and contingent on "a supportive environment that offers opportunities for success." The study, a ludicrous exercise in circular reasoning, became the foundation of the National Council on Self-Esteem. Betcha didn't know we had one of these councils to help us run our lives.

Somebody Help Gloria Steinem

In her recent book *Revolution from Within: A Book of Self-Esteem,* Ms. Steinem describes her own self-esteem deficiency, telling us that in spite of her accomplishments, good looks, outer strength, and international acclaim, she still suffers "inner feelings of incompleteness, emptiness, self-doubt, and self-hatred." While her candor is admirable, it is possible that she has missed the boat on the main point of her feminist cause, which is to help women get more satisfaction from their lives. While she gains competency and political power, as feminism would have it, she feels vulnerable, ashamed, and unhappy with herself. Her partisans and followers might consider taking a rational shortcut to self-esteem that would spare them the disappointment of bringing about social change and still feeling like underdogs.

In her article "The Road to Self-Esteem" *(Ladies' Home Journal,* January 1993), Claire Safran reviews the Steinem book and presents a researched prescription of helpful hints for gaining self-esteem. This article, which reflects the current state of understanding of self-esteem in America, reworks old material that actually causes and perpetuates problems with low self-esteem, depression, and the other difficulties Ms. Steinem complains of. It is worth noting that Ms. Safran supports her recommendations with materials written by psychiatrist Donald Nathanson, M.D. *Caveat emptor.* Here is a synopsis, italicized, of her recommendations on "how to feel better about yourself." (When you have read our chapter "Our Unmiraculous Recovery from Fatness," it might be interesting to review these items.) Rational responses follow.

1. *Take a personal inventory, listing your positive and negative traits, your strengths and weaknesses. This is supposed to help you avoid concluding that you are a total jerk. When you fail in the future, you can be specific about the failure in question and weigh this against your competencies and conclude that you are not all bad or completely incompetent. The failure in question was only one bad trait among many positives.*

This is probably the *worst* thing to tell someone suffering from poor self-esteem and the resulting depression and social inhibition. The idea that one *could* be a bad or inferior person—one who is unworthy and who should hate oneself—is entirely supported in this recommendation. By developing a "good girl list" and a "bad girl list," the irrational idea of *variable personal worth* is dignified and played into—that is, when you are "bad," think of all the "good" you have done in order to cancel out your badness.

2. *Be realistic. Your personal best is good enough. For example, if you play tennis with a superior player and lose, you don't have to berate yourself if you have played your best.*

The irrational idea here is that self-esteem, or what we will call self-acceptance, is conferred on one when he or she has made the best effort. Is there any evidence in the universe to support this profoundly absurd contention? People who play tennis to the best of their ability are inherently more worthwhile than players who slough off?

3. *Don't be materialistic. Don't measure yourself by the things you have.*

Sounds good, eh? But read on.

Genuine self-esteem has interpersonal and spiritual yardsticks. Ask yourself: What do I have to give to this world? Whom do I love, and who loves me? Am I in touch with a sense of purpose or a Higher Power?

Whoops. Now the doctor tells us that self-esteem depends on other people, and that loving and being loved is a condition of self-esteem. And to make his psychiatric stew more palatable, he adds a dash of "spirituality" and a new, mysterious element, "contact with a Higher Power." Could he possibly be referring to God? Is this what doctors know about?

4. *Imagine success. Start each morning imagining doing everything right. Even if you're not feeling confident, act as if you are. Believe it.*

Well. In addition to being loved by other people, not making mistakes, counting your positive traits, and being in touch with a Higher Power, we now find that success is a vital element in self-esteem. It seems that Dr. Nathanson understands that the prospect of an adult human being making a mistake is a living horror and therefore must be neutralized with mental fictions such as imagining a perfect day ahead. Goodness. No wonder so many people have low self-esteem.

5. *Focus on your accomplishments. Each evening, review your successes during that day, big or little. Look in the mirror and read your accomplishments aloud.*

What a horror imperfection must be. Count every little success, look in the mirror, and tell yourself how much you esteem yourself because of your personal functioning. Functional people are more esteemable, more worthy, than dysfunctional people. From which Reich does this kind of thinking come?

6. *Be positive. In divorce, self-esteem sinks. But you can make a list of people who think you're worthwhile. And you can remind yourself that*

if one man loved you enough to marry you, another man can love you in the future.

Don't be realistic; be positive. What is the doctor's problem with reality? Does divorce cause low self-esteem? Or is it the opposite? Why would one reject oneself because he or she is being rejected in divorce? Why depend on other people to believe you are worthwhile? What's wrong with just believing in oneself regardless of what others think? Do women need to be loved by a man? Is that what defines a woman's worth to herself?

7. *Meditate. Call up your inner child. Ask her what hurts. Is she ashamed? In your meditation, imagine giving your inner child what she needs—a hug, a loving word, reassurance. Gloria Steinem says, "It's never too late to have a happy childhood."*

It seems that children are more worthy of love and esteem than adults, according to the rating scheme presented in this *LHJ* article. Don't love yourself for what you are—imagine yourself as a child. Children are innocent—you are not. What a disturbing message of hopelessness is given here. Gloria Steinem would do better to convey that it is clearly too late for any adult to have a happy childhood if one did not actually have one. But even so, one may be happy it's over, and then quite efficiently *grow up,* by just loving oneself for no other reason than that it feels so much better than hating oneself. Public figures owe this kind of encouragement to themselves as well as to the millions of very important people who respect their work.

Over and over, Americans—women in particular—are fed the above kind of nonsense. We are made to feel as if life is a stage for proving we are good, that we must succeed to feel good about ourselves, that we must be loved by someone of the opposite sex to feel validated, that we must look good to feel good, that innocence is the antidote to shame. Self-esteem is a sickness, not a cure. The only sure antidote is in unconditional self-acceptance, a birthright in the sense that we are all capable of self-love. But self-esteem cannot be earned except in a fleeting way by success and by competency, and it cannot be conferred by the opinions—even the loving opinions—of others. Like all freedoms, self-acceptance is staked out and authoritatively claimed against the claims of others, against the pervasive social forces that threaten each person with self-annihilation through low self-esteem.

I'm gonna get me sumpin' good!
—the Feast Beast

CHAPTER 3

Voices and Visions

Fat people hear voices. But then, so does everyone else. In the brain there is a noisemaker. As an old saying goes, "Everybody's got one." In the normal consciousness of us all, there are voices, usually sounding like our own. In our "mind's ear" we can literally hear ourselves talking to ourselves. You can hear one of your own voices right now as you read these words. It may sound something like yours, or it may sound the way you imagine this writer would sound. Our mind's ear can also produce a seemingly infinite variety of sound effects, such as birds, surf, explosions, engines, and music. Quite often we provide mental pictures to go along with the sound effects. We humans lead such rich inner lives!

Our voices express our perceptions of reality, our ideas and beliefs about life and ourselves, and our evaluations of experience and circumstance. Together, each person's perceptions, beliefs, ideas, and evaluations comprise what we will call a philosophy of life. Everybody has one of these, too. And while everyone's philosophy is somewhat different from everyone else's, there are also certain similarities and traits worth noting.

Long ago, the philosophers Aristotle and Plato described their visions of man in the universe, and to this day these two schools of thought divide the discourse on human affairs into two very broad categories: the Aristotelian rational and the Platonic irrational. In philosophy, these are two main trunks of thought to which the rest of human discourse can be traced and classified. To (overly) simplify, Aristotle perceived reality as knowable and humans as essentially rational beings—knowers and doers. To him, A=A—that is, things are pretty much as they appear to be. To Plato, reality is largely unknowable except as revealed esoterically to a learned class; the average person cannot trust his senses and ability to reason; in other words, A≠A. People seem inclined to one viewpoint or the other, depending on early learning, education, or perhaps the dominance of one cerebral hemisphere over the other —innate disposition. Skepticism is Aristotelian, faith is Platonic. RR is very Aristotelian, AA and OA are very Platonic.

Although each of us is inclined toward one or the other viewpoint, we all are also naturally disposed to both rational *and* irrational thinking. Our folklore is robust with rational gems such as "There's no use crying over spilt milk" and "Sticks and stones may break my bones, but names will never hurt me." But we are also handed down homilies that are at best unprovable, misleading, and sometimes downright false and emotionally disturbing, such as "No man is an island; everyone needs to be loved," or, as often seen on Valentine's Day cards, "Before I met you I was nothing; now I am everything." Other examples are (in an adolescent love song) "I want you, I need you, I love you" (as if "need" means "want" or "love"), "Your love is lifting me higher" (otherwise I don't think very much of myself), and in defense of theism, "There are no atheists in foxholes," and "If there were no God, we would have to invent Him." Living as we do in a largely irrational society, our inner voices take on ideas and beliefs that we accept, because of their prevalence and popularity, without critical analysis. In his *Reason and Emotion in Psychotherapy* and *A New Guide for Rational Living,* the works upon which Rational Recovery is based, Albert Ellis enumerates a dozen or so "common irrational ideas which cause and perpetuate emotional disturbance." He shows, and research bears out, that disturbed, unhappy people can help themselves considerably by disputing their own irrational ideas and then replacing them with rational ideas that, *by definition,* are objectively true and serve their enlightened self-interest.

Before examining the common ideas that perpetuate overeating and the weight loss relapse cycle, we had better acknowledge some significant differences between fat (overweight) people and persons of ordinary dimensions and appetites. Foremost, overeaters suffer impaired cognition and judgment while hungry. While persons with normal appetites harbor a balance of rational and irrational ideas, overeaters are profoundly irrational, or unreasoning, when it comes to the ingestion of food. Because food acts directly on and deeply within the midbrain, and because food acts on the mid-brain's pleasure centers in its paradoxical way, overeaters are at a severe disadvantage in protecting themselves from the regrettable results of overindulgence. Overeaters are powerfully conditioned to the "quick fix" of another food binge because the results are so swift and usually so immediately gratifying; it is fair to say that overeaters live on a roller coaster of pain and pleasure. Pleasure becomes progressively more associated with food, even though food is also the indirect cause of the underlying pain. Conse-quently, overeaters devise a personal philosophy that is aimed at providing an unlimited and convenient supply of concentrated and tasty food. This *fatness* philosophy is a subset of the person's over-all philosophy, so that he or she may function quite sanely and rationally in many significant ways and yet have firm convictions regarding food that seem to deny the presence of human intelli-gence.

In fact, there is an animal, or beastly, quality to the inner voice that regularly dominates the consciousness of overeaters. It is a voice—an *addictive* voice—that exists only to obtain more food and it is always hungry whether its host, the overeater, is or isn't. Its singular purpose is to obtain as many fattening substances as possible by having its host place them in the mouth and swallow them. Under the influence of hunger, anger, depression, festivity, success, or just plain boredom, "It," this "Thing," or "Beast," becomes amplified and, operating on the immediate, biological pleasure principle, "It" drowns out other voices of moderation and prudence and effectively controls the decisions, judgments, and behavior of its fat host.

Just prior to and during food binges, your addictive voice (we may call this inner voice your Feast Beast) is in complete control of your motor and language faculties and capable of authentic gluttony. Upon satiation, your rational voice returns, asking, "What did I do?" along with common irrational ideas such as, "Oh, what a worm I am for having screwed up once again," and "I've *got* to stop overeating so I can feel like a decent human being," and "I'm *powerless* over this thing; I guess there's no hope for me." Heedless and insatiable, the Feast Beast soon intrudes with, "Have a bite to eat; it'll take the edge off."

Your rational voice, which happens to be *you,* wavers and subsides in the presence of desire for comfort. And so the cycle continues, with the Feast Beast always having the last word, as well as the ideal solution to any problem—another little bite to eat. It can speak in many tones and is capable of great cunning in its pursuit of calories. It makes and breaks relationships by choosing only those associates who are somehow compatible with its culinary agenda and by spawning envy or resentment toward those who are not inclined toward excess. The Feast Beast seethes and rails at those who would attempt to discourage its host's compulsive overeating, whether it be a spouse, a boss, a neighbor, a doctor, or a therapist. All of the above are declared potential enemies to be tricked, manipulated, faced down, or avoided. Its own survival comes first, even before that of its host, and survival means *megacalories,* not just the nutrition that sustains life, normal health, and vigor.

The fact that its host is growing huge and suffering back problems, sexual unhappiness, heart disease, social embarrassment, high blood pressure, marital conflict, or failure of the joints in no way deters the Feast Beast from seeking ever more food to appease its unending hunger. To the Feast Beast, the human body is only a device to go and fetch food, for as long as it can function. The Feast Beast listens to the rational voices that challenge its firm control over the host and then plays word games to destroy any resolve just made. "You can lose weight any time you want to, but not just now. You can go overboard just a little. You're not really out of control, you're just hungry, and that means you have to eat something, so why not make it something really good? It's time for something really good now. Now. See what's in the refrigerator. Check the cupboard; there's probably something great you've forgotten about. You really need something nutritious and tasty!" So the host has a high-calorie treat. And the host, you, can *hear* the Feast Beast saying "The-r-r-re! That's gooood. Ohhh, how wonderful! That really hits the spot. You deserve this from time to time. This is an important part of life, to feel so good this way."

Deprived of its nourishment, such as when one goes on a diet, the Feast Beast loses some of its strength. But it does not die; after struggling against the host's self-control, it collapses into a semi-sleep. But it does not sleep deeply. It lies in the dimness of preconsciousness with one eye half open, waiting for the chance to catch the host unaware at a choice moment. Then the Feast Beast will suggest, in the most endearing terms, "Once again, friend, it is time for something really, really good, and lots of it!"

There is no such thing as the Feast Beast, of course. It is merely a metaphor to illustrate the exaggerated, extremely irrational, specialized self-talk with which the compulsive overeater relates to food. These thought sequences may continue for months and years after overeating has been stopped, but like any habit, the Feast Beast gradually loses strength.

It is quite useful for any compulsive overeater to recognize that there is some very poor-quality, self-destructive thinking going on with regard to food, thinking that can be identified, categorized as ego-alien ("That's not me!"), challenged, and corrected. When you learn the origins of this voice, in "The Structural Model of Food Addiction," later in this chapter, you may find it quite easy to dissociate from it when you are tempted to binge.

The following pages show *exactly* how to resist the impulse to eat at the wrong times, to eat the wrong things, or to eat too much. You may be among those who find the BEAST device the keystone for weight loss and weight control. The BEAST device is internal and under your control. In other words, you can easily learn to dominate the Feast Beast that demands ever more calories, and demands that each and every bite you take tastes heavenly. If you care for yourself, you will not fail yourself.

The Gimmick That Can Change Your Life

In Rational Recovery (RR) there is a special memory device, BEAST, that allows you to gain control quickly and effectively over your impulses to overeat, provided the undesirability of over-eating is clearly established in your mind. Your appetite for fatten-ing food supersedes satiation, transcends social disapproval, and proves "irresistible" when you are trying to eat sensibly. Some-times it seems that you have *no defense* against the desire to eat. This is just more fatness philosophy and simply is not so, for the BEAST device is an *excellent* defense once you get the hang of it. Here it is:

THE BEAST OF RATIONAL RECOVERY

Bingeing opportunity

Enemy recognition

Accuse the Feast Beast of malice

Self-control and self-worth reminders

Treasure your health and happiness, the "Big Plan"

You may call upon the above concept any time the desire to overindulge in food occurs. It has the advantages of simplicity and a high degree of relevance to the immediate circumstances. Any idea of inappropriate eating emanates from an irrational ego-alien source, one that can be conceptualized as an ugly, dread enemy that cares nothing for the health, welfare, success, happiness, or even the survival of you, its rational host. "It" is a beast in every sense except reality, for, of course, the "Feast Beast" is only a product of our fertile imaginations.

   "Bingeing opportunity" is any circumstance or time when you are considering eating incorrectly, whether it is the wrong food, the wrong amount, or the wrong time. It could be at a wedding, a certain holiday or anniversary, a time of day when you are unaccustomed to eating, an unexpected event such as being handed a creamy dessert when out of town and away from familiar people and routines, when passing a fast-food joint, when a serious misfortune occurs, or one of those "out of the blue" impulses to have a bite to eat. Sometimes overeaters who have been slimmed down for years will start contemplating future binges; this kind of thinking also originates from the Feast Beast.

Thoughts about any prospective actions (especially eating actions) come in pairs. This dualism can be seen in just about any action, from the simplest—such as going to bed or getting up in the morning (should I or shouldn't I?), to the most complex—such as getting married or starting college (should I or shouldn't I?). There seems to be some degree of ambivalence about all our decisions. The overeater is subject to two mental commands: "Eat!" and "Don't eat!" A lapse is when the "Eat!" voice prevails and is obeyed.

"**Enemy recognition**" is the RR self-awareness that defines *any thinking that supports incorrect eating* as the "enemy." During the early months of recovery, recognition of the "enemy" cognition is difficult, because you are accustomed to the idea that "All of my thoughts are my own and therefore are accorded equal merit." Just *recognizing* the Feast Beast (up to its old tricks) is sufficient to put it on the defensive. Simple recognition of BEAST-ly ideas has a sudden dampening effect on the impulse to eat wrongly. At the point of recognition, you are suddenly *thinking about your thinking* and therefore exercising a *higher order of consciousness* about the use of food. Recognition allows you to see that rather than being powerless, you have only been obeying a dominant mental command to eat incorrectly. Control of your eating behavior is now within your grasp.

RR group meetings, if they are available, reinforce recognition of any ideas, imagery, or voices that suggest incorrect eating, and participants' current reasons for wanting to slim down are frequently reviewed. The goal in RR is to become *extremely self-*

conscious of any thinking that supports overeating, in either the long term or especially the short term.

"Feast Beast" ideations can be subtle, as the following example shows. Suppose you are invited to a social occasion where there is going to be considerable eating of rich, gourmet foods, and there are also some distinct advantages to attending (business contacts, someone you like will be there, or you just want to have fun). You would really like to go, but remembering the great importance of eating correctly and recalling that you have often given in to the impulse to binge in the past, you may decide to sit at home instead. On the surface this would seem like a prudent decision, one that serves your rational self-interest. Not necessarily so.

What's going on here is that you may very well be perpetuating the old irrational idea (one that *every* overeater is supposed to believe!) that *"If I go to this party where all my friends are, the temptation to binge may be so overwhelming that I will inevitably end up eating everything in sight and ruining my cherished diet. Because I am an overeater, or one who is overweight, I am powerless at certain times to refrain from eating wrongly. Therefore, since I may become powerless at the upcoming party, I had better not even go."* If you can imagine a clever omnivorous creature planting the seeds for further eating binges, you will also see that concealed in this seemingly prudent viewpoint is the prophetic root of weight loss relapse—the idea that "I am powerless over my decisions to eat correctly or incorrectly." The idea of attending the party may even be accompanied with anxiety stemming from the idea that "I want to go to the party so much that I may actually go, and if I do, I'll end up on a food binge that will last for weeks, and that will be catastrophic and awful!"

We think in pictures as well as sentences, so along with the above self-talk you may also "see" yourself succumbing to the impulse to gluttonize at the party. You may see glorious visions of pastries, sweet cream beverages, and hot apple tarts through your mind's eye. These visions of heavenly indulgence are actually *rehearsals of weight loss relapse,* so that the "Feast Beast" is, in essence, *preparing* you for the time when a relapse will occur. You can just as easily, and certainly more rationally, imagine a more desirable scenario, a rehearsal of *nonrelapse,* in which you imagine yourself firmly and comfortably refusing rich and colorful incorrect food intake—and in living color!

"<u>A</u>ccuse the Feast Beast of malice." Various dissociative (distancing) techniques can be used, and there is room here for considerable creativity. Some people find anger toward the imaginary enemy to be effective and appropriate, and others find sarcasm and humor fitting ways of prevailing over the monolithic mentality that would accept suffering, poor health, personal disfigurement, social and vocational discrimination, sexual frustration, and even death as an even trade for unlimited doughnuts. Members learn to respond actively and assertively to the coaxings of the Feast Beast, typically by answering, "I hear my Feast Beast telling me to eat one cookie after the other. I see images of doing it (I see its video), and I know what it's up to. It wants want me to ruin my diet so it can get all the calories it wants, but I'm not going to cooperate. It wants me to think I'm powerless over its persuasion and give in and eat stupidly. It is crude and ugly, but I have the upper hand. Suffer, plead, and beg all you want, O Feast Beast, but you'll not get a single calorie from me until dinner three hours from now. I reject the Feast Beast because it will destroy me if it can." I (L.T.) have sometimes chuckled at the absurd ploys I hear from my internalized self-sentences that suggest an eventual food binge. With time, it is hard to take those ideas seriously.

"<u>S</u>elf-control and self-worth reminders" refer to specific rational antidotes to poor impulse control and self-worth problems, described in Chapter 1 as "Central Ideas of the Philosophy of Fatness." For example, some defeat the Feast Beast by holding their hands in front of their face and simply remembering that they have complete voluntary control over their muscles and can easily refuse to move their extremities until the Feast Beast is finally faced down. In RR you will find that you can make yourself feel good even when hungry just by thinking well of yourself; you need not change in any other way to do so. Ironically, we think well of ourselves for the same reason we used to overeat—to feel good. We do not slim down to think well of ourselves; it is because we like or value ourselves that we eat correctly. Self-worth reminders simply express unconditional self-acceptance and the idea that to overeat or binge would be betraying a friend, oneself.

"**Treasure your health and happiness**" simply means taking an overview and reaffirming the intrinsic value of eating correctly, focusing on how many of life's other pleasures can be achieved through moderation in diet. This will bolster your commitment to permanent change, or the "Big Plan."

Addictive Voice Recognition Training (AVRT)

It is a happy occasion when the words describing something also result in an acronym that has a related meaning. That is what happened in Rational Recovery, when our concepts of self-control were described as the task of learning to recognize the thoughts that support self-intoxication or overeating. Our important goal is to avert lapses into excessive or unnecessary eating and relapses into unbridled gluttony. It is not an easy task to become self-aware in this way, and it does take some personal discipline, effort, and practice. Therefore, recovery from fatness is a process of training oneself to recognize the ideations that perpetuate eating disorders.

Rational Recovery utilizes rational-emotive behavior therapy (REBT) as a foundation for effective living and for solving emotional problems, but RR also presents a intense focus on food-specific thoughts called AVRT. AVRT departs from the ABC process of rational-emotive behavior therapy, which you will learn more about in a later chapter, in that we conceptualize a primal motivation behind eating disorders—that is, the Feast Beast. AVRT is not simply a variation on the ABC theme of REBT fame, but is a specialized technique for defeating addictive behavior. As you read you may notice the parallels as well as qualitative differences between the BEAST device and the ABC paradigm.

The Beauty of the Beast

The Feast Beast we speak of in RR is not the Cookie Monster of TV fame. That charming character is far too cute to be of any therapeutic use to those of us who compulsively overeat. The Feast Beast of RR is a deadly serious entity of your own creation that personifies the biological drives that are an integrated part of your human nature. Our use of the imaginary entity is to bring to our awareness lines of conscious thought that otherwise cannot be identified, remembered, or changed. If you will recall your last food binge, you will notice that your only recollection of thinking during the entire binge, which may have been hours long, is after you started to become satiated. Until then, it very likely seems to you that you were under some spell, as if you weren't really thinking at all, transfixed, on automatic pilot. You may vaguely remember going through the motions of preparing the food, but you will have great difficulty remembering anything you thought as you veered toward relapse and then consummated your desire to eat. You "came to your senses" all too late, just as you began to feel the glut of excess. And then you came on strong, with exasperation and guilt: "Oh, now look what I've done. I've really blown it. Why do I always do this? Why? Oh, why? Oh, what an idiot I am!" Those thoughts, the self-downing, hopeless, self-blaming ones, you can remember in vivid detail. "How could I have done that?" you may ask later. "What was I even *thinking* to end up on another binge?"

There are three equally useless and preposterous theories that attempt to explain what drives us to dietary excess. The first is psychoanalytical—the Freudian school of thought. It views humans as being under the control of unconscious forces, an unconscious mind separate from the being we think we are and that contradicts our conscious desires and intentions. Someone late for an appointment is said to *want* unconsciously to be late, perhaps as a way of expressing anger to the other party, or to guarantee failure and ensure self-punishment. Overeaters, along the same line of psychoanalytic thought, are said to be unconsciously doing all kinds of things, such as avoiding sex, getting even with Mother, acting out pregnancy frustrations, attempting to regain a lost childhood, or trying to compensate for some real or imagined impoverishment. These explanations not only take the problem out of the overeater's hands, but they are also far too clever. They glamorize the mundane far more than they add to understanding, and they fail to offer any useful means for losing weight. Too often these fancy psychoanalytic interpretations become powerful deterrents to personal growth as they strongly support the irrational idea that the past is a potent determiner of one's present difficulties. In RR these explanations of why one overeats are regarded as "excuses."

The second theory that attempts to explain compulsive overeating is the "no-mind behaviorism" that has attained some popularity in recent years. The idea here is that a stimulus leads to a response, as with Pavlov's dog or Skinner's rats and pigeons. While stripped-down behaviorism has made valuable contributions in some areas, the concepts are often used by overeaters to support their continued bingeing: "My overeating is caused by such-and-such," or "My overeating is a conditioned response to _____." This is stimulus-response (S-R) thinking, which ignores the central part that cognition (thinking) plays in determining our emotions and behavior. It also removes any effective handle on the problem. Fortunately, we are considerably more thoughtful than pigeons. A variation on S-R, added later to account for different responses to the same stimulus, is S-O-R, where O stands for "organism." "Something's going on in there," early behaviorists said as they pondered the human skull. And that leads us to rational-emotive behavior therapy (REBT), devised by Albert Ellis, Ph.D., who in the early 1950s transposed S-O-R into the ABC paradigm that is now a standard psychotherapeutic method taught in most American universities. As a humanistic approach based in scientific thought, REBT has been widely criticized as a refutation of "traditional (irrational) values," but it has been even more widely *copied* by more image-conscious theorists who, after all, would like their professional colleagues to put in a good day's work at the clinic practicing "cognitive-behavioral therapy" and actually help people to overcome their persistent problems. The fact that lower animal species were observed to form the conclusions of a behavioral psychology for humans should raise some serious questions.

The third theory that "explains" personal vice is the devil theory, still devoutly believed in by large numbers, even in these modern times. If you believe that some external entity is making you overeat and you are unwilling to reexamine this portion of your religious faith, then it would make some sense to consult with clergy. RR is a program of personal change that is separate from, but not contradictory to, most major world religions. An ongoing study done by Harvard University Medical School found that 27 percent of people who had made use of *The Small Book* (Delacorte Press, 1992) in recovery from chemical dependency believe in God or a Supreme Being.

Some RR members ask, "Isn't the Beast idea basically the same thing as the devil theory?" The answer here is a very definite "no." There is no connection in RR to any realm other than reality—the material world. The devil is an invisible being that is said to exist *apart from* human beings and is said to be responsible for everything that goes bad in the world. That is an entirely different concept from the Beast of RR, which is only an *imaginary* entity that *personifies* certain biologically driven thoughts. It is no accident that in theology the devil is sometimes also called "the Beast," because some religious ideas of "evil" identify our biological, animal-like drives, most notably sex, but also aggression. As with the Cookie Monster, the devil concept has some fringe overlap with the Beast of RR, but all three of these entities have very fundamental differences. To sum up this issue, let us say that it is irrational to *believe* in Santa Claus, but quite rational to *imagine* that jolly character.

People have been overcoming patterns of self-defeat for thousands of years, and it is quite likely that most of these people have approached their problems along the lines of the Beast concept. This is really nothing new. The Beast of RR has an advantage over the Higher Power of twelve-step programs because it is of our own creation and therefore under our own control. The Feast Beast device is more dependable than Higher Powers that are often fickle, unreliable, easily forgotten about, or that disappear just when we "need" them most. Remember, you cannot really make up a Higher Power; he, she, or it is really out there—or he, she, or it isn't. It's a matter of belief. Moreover, the Beast of RR is not a device for externally imposed "morality," as are religious icons such as the devil, Satan, God, Jesus, saints, rescuing and punitive deities, and the like. The Beast of RR is only a device that people may intelligently construct as a way to pursue selfishly their own self-defined patterns of abstinence or moderation, as their own painful experiences suggest. Selecting a self-improvement project— for example, overeating or alcohol dependence—is a very personal decision, and there is no reason why anyone should, ought to, or must refrain from such pleasurable indulgences. However, when one is finally unwilling to accept the painful consequences of some habitual behavior and is finally ready to get serious about the prob- lem, he or she may choose to call a specialized RR Beast into existence. It is in the spirit of independence and self-determination that the beauty of the Beast lies.

For example, many people, as you are probably acutely aware, eat large amounts of whatever they choose and never gain a pound, nor do they even suffer an ill effect. Those people would have little use for a Feast Beast. The large majority of people can drink alco- hol appropriately and without serious consequences, but about 10 percent of the general population develop a profound dependency on alcohol and suffer devastating consequences. Those individuals would benefit greatly from developing Booze Beast, as described in *The Small Book.* People wanting to stop smoking cigarettes will be dealing with Smoky the Beast.

What about the other "addictions" that are said to be sweeping America, such as relationship addiction and sex addiction? Here also, the Beast can be employed, but the problem is that those patterns of excess or self-defeat are not really addictions, in the sense that heroin or alcohol are addictions. Nor is food an addic- tion in the sense that food has intoxicating, mind-altering proper- ties. The term "addiction" has been corrupted in recent years in the literature of New Age and twelve-step spiritual healing pro- grams so that it has become a buzzword for *any* bad habit, *any* pattern of self-defeat, or *any* morally tinged social vice.

The Latin root for "addiction" is "dict," meaning, "say," with the prefix, "ad," meaning "toward." With this understanding, overeating can be viewed as an addiction. Overeaters say, "Yes, bring it to me" to food and are impaired in their ability to say "no" to food.

Likewise, persons who have become habituated to masturbation, promiscuous sexual encounters, or deviant practices so that there are unacceptable risks or consequences, may also be said to be "addicted." But there is a problem when we view all self-defeating behavior as "addiction." From a rational viewpoint, no sexual act is intrinsically evil or wicked, but in its *context* it may be unethical, coercive, illegal, injurious, exploitive, or carry the risk of pregnancy or infection. Since they are biologically driven, sexual desires can attain a compulsive character not unlike excessive drinking and overeating, leading one to undesirable outcomes and consequences. Although promiscuous people may "say yes" to sex in a self-defeating way, that does not mean an addiction is present. That would make anything that is lots of fun an addiction.

So, one may ask, is there a "Sex Beast" cavorting in everyone's head, demanding endless fornication in the streets? Not at all; to view a natural appetite of the human body in that light is sexual moralism and quite irrational. But anyone choosing to modify his or her sexual behavior as a matter of self-interest (not self-worth!) might do well to start listening to his or her irrational self-sentences and monitoring the mental imagery that invariably precedes the unwanted sexual behavior. If one's sexual behavior repeatedly produces unacceptable consequences in spite of attempts to avoid trouble, then creating a personal "Sex Beast" idea would be a simple and probably effective approach.

Regardless of which Beast is under discussion, they all have much in common. Here are some Beast parameters:

1. They are symbolic figments of our own fertile imaginations (and not of any external authority) that characterize or symbolize the appetites, desires, impulses, and urges that get us into trouble.
2. They use our intelligence, language faculties, and the

faculty of voluntary movement to continue the undesirable behavior.

3. They thrive in an irrational psychological environment.
4. They speak to the mind's ear and show enticing pictures to the mind's eye.
5. They are able to change form, using various vocal tones, attitudes, and strategies in the struggle to consummate desire.
6. They revel in the company of other Beasts with the same priority—that is, "commingling of Beasts."
7. They fear death by deprivation and require "that one thing" to survive.
8. They are ruthless in pursuit of food and will go to any length to get it, even though we, the rational hosts, may have to suffer or even die in the process.
9. They are inferior to the human intellect and need not be feared but only objectively recognized.
10. They often become silent upon recognition, yield readily to reason, and practically always lose strength when their primitive demands are not met.
11. They maintain power through concealment and *seem to be us.*
12. They *cannot tolerate* exposure and rational evaluation.
13. They blunder by using pronouns that can expose them.
14. Once mastered, they don't die, but only half sleep, watching patiently for any opportunity to revive themselves with a hit of "you know what."
15. But they are easily identified and may be easily squelched.
16. They may become permanent features of our rich inner lives and are not easily forgotten.

The Feast Beast, once you get the hang of it, will always be at your disposal, and you need only learn to recognize its urgings. Once that is learned, you will find that relapse is preceded by a great deal of *premeditation,* and that overeating is the result of a series of highly conscious *decisions.* When you recall your last binge, you will be able, at last, to remember exactly how you relapsed, and how you decided to overeat. You will *remember* the voice that kicks in when you are hungry, and you will be able to recall its tone, the words it used, and also the pictures the Feast Beast may have flashed before your mind's eye to get the salivation really going. Now, for a change, you will be able to *learn from relapse,* something heretofore impossible because your overeating has for decades been shrouded in mystery of the medical or psychoanalytic types.

Seeing Through the Disease Model of "Food Addiction"

Professionals and students of nutrition are currently taught that the cause of overeating lies in the complex, inherited physiology of the human body. They explain the mysteries of obesity in pseudo-scientific jargon as follows: Infants are born with a genetic predisposition to food addiction. Then they are fed many different foods, many of which contain addictive substances, especially sugar. The disease is triggered by eating sugar, the child becomes a food addict, and at that time emotional growth stops. The addicted child is unable to mature normally and grows fatter, finally becoming alienated from peers. The fat cells in the addicted child become larger and more numerous, so that even if the child loses weight during puberty, adolescence, or early adulthood, this is only a reprieve from lifelong food addiction and obesity. The food addict's personality is malformed because of active addiction during the child's formative years. Therefore the adult is inherently impaired in his or her ability to function in important roles and especially in controlling the intake of food. Eating becomes an obsession around which one structures one's life, and all social relationships are distorted by the disease of food addiction.

This kind of thinking does *nothing* for people with serious eating disorders. Because overweight people are struggling fruitlessly against their compulsion to eat excessively, they become discouraged, desperate, and extremely vulnerable to ideas of incompetence, powerlessness, and debilitating disease. The disease model of food addiction is, well, like a disease. It breeds hopelessness and despair, and a perfect opportunity to yield to the path of least resistance—more food bingeing to relieve the pain of being overweight.

This "biogenic" theory of overeating has permeated thinking in American addiction care to such an extent that overweight people themselves come to believe that they are inherently defective and incompetent to lose extra pounds and keep them off. Textbooks on addiction abound with research studies from around the world that show how the disease of obesity and food addiction runs in families, and twin studies are presented that show very convincingly that genetics plays a very central role in the development of eating disorders. So what else is new? If one eats too much he or she is diseased, and the reason that person eats so much is that he or she has a disease. But the idea of addiction as disease has gone farther than this simple, absurd paradigm.

Here is the latest manifestation of disease thinking: *People who engage in self-defeating behavior are addicted to themselves.* That's correct. According to the latest educational materials and publishing trends in professional periodicals, addiction is the common ingredient in human disturbance, and practically all human problems may now be regarded as manifestations of addiction. For example, gambling is regarded as a disease wherein one is risking money to alter one's brain chemistry, to get the "rush" of winning against odds—that is, "getting high on adrenaline."

Codependency was recently described in a periodical of the nursing profession, *Focus on Critical Care* (April 1992), as addiction to one's own body chemicals. "The brain is a giant pharmaceutical factory that manufactures powerful mind-altering chemicals," the authors cite, and addiction is "courting the chemical or behavior that fits the individual style of coping—that is, a pharmacological defense mechanism." The article, in its weird-world style, goes on, "The addictive personality, therefore, is a *result,* not the cause, of addiction." There! It is complete! Salvation is at hand! We are addicted to *ourselves*—our serotonin, our dopamine, our epinephrine! *"Oh, gimme some o' dat brain juice! Who's buyin'?"*

But this is only the beginning of a brave new logic that began thousands of years ago. Listen to how this article continues: "Addiction is a single disease; what differs is the individual's substance of choice. Cross-addictions support this, such as when a recovering alcoholic substitutes sugar for alcohol. Then there are the process addictions such as accumulating money, sex, gambling, religion, work, and worry." Three addictive personality types correspond to three specific neurotransmitters, "people pleasers seek the high of serotonin, novelty-seekers engage in activities that release dopamine, and those who are reward-dependent will seek the release of norepinephrine."

Shucks. When I (J.T.) was a kid, playing cards was a sin. And we all knew what that meant. And masturbation was a sin, too. And so was dancing, and lots of other fun things. As a young man, I thought I had it bad as a skeptical kid in a religious town. I'm glad I was young then and not now. As a kid today I would be a norepinephrine junkie and see a social worker once a week. *Sick.* Sin is far more fun than being sick.

I (L.T.) heard an overweight woman say that even if she lost weight, she would still be returning to an addictive relationship with a man, and she also certainly planned to continue playing bingo to some extent. These, she mused in her addictive mode of thought, are addictions that trigger the release of adrenaline and other chemicals, and since she was certainly suffering from addictive disease, she would actually accomplish very little by abstaining from food. I asked her why she wanted to lose weight in the first place, and she said with deadpan sincerity, "To escape the pain I brought on by escaping pain caused by overeating." Life was too painful, and recovery seemed wrought with endless struggle with her biology. What a mess she was in.

She believed that recovery from addiction is futile. She described her boyfriend, who liked motorcycles and downhill skiing, as being addicted to adrenaline. She explained, "Adrenaline hits his blood just like crack cocaine! All addicts love the rush, and he's like a common junkie. He gave up alcohol but now he's doing the same thing with his own endorphins. That's cross-addiction in my book."

Well. It seems that crooked thinking from the professional crowd gets around to the general population pretty quickly. People, in spite of their reservations, still do take professionals seriously. She was convinced that they were both addicted to their body juice—to their own chemistry—and what they did for fun, including sports and sex, were manifestations of addictive disease.

She had forgotten what life is about. She had given up on recovering from her problems, and in life she saw an endless addiction opera. She hated the pain of obesity, but she could find no reason to stop it except to reduce her pain; she had no hope for the good, and no plan to be happy. Without a positive reason to lose weight, she will remain obese, and have a joyless relationship with a man who loves to have fun. To her, fun is sick, and joy is a New Age sin. This is the oldest racket going—be miserable to be good. Make self-deprivation a virtue. Then she'll sense that there's no difference between good, clean fun—whether it's sex, gambling, painting pictures, or riding a motorcycle—and eating herself into oblivion. Hopeless attitudes like these will prevent people from undertaking self-improvement.

The Structural Model of Food Addiction

To attack a long-standing overweight problem, many people will find it very useful and productive to redraw the map of food addiction. The following conception of food addiction not only describes the problem in simple terms but also provides an understanding of how to achieve control over one's eating and body weight.

At the end of the spinal cord is a bulb, the brain stem, and upon that structure rests what is now called the midbrain (old brain). Millennia ago, before evolution brought us our nicely folded and convoluted outer layer of gray matter, the neocortex (new brain), the midbrain would have been called *the* brain. But, of course, the absence of an intelligent, language-generating neocortex during those simpler times precluded such a conception as the brain. The midbrain, however, in spite of whatever else it lacked, was and still is an amazingly efficient entity that is geared toward physical survival of individuals and of the human species. It is well suited to life in the jungle, where, as the late Robert Ingersoll remarked, "Every mouth is a slaughterhouse, and every stomach a tomb." The midbrain is the site of strong, compelling appetites for the necessities of life itself—food, sex, and safety, as well as the cunning, resourcefulness, and efficiency for obtaining those goals. The midbrain, with its hard-wired programs of survival, has been enormously successful in sustaining the human species over the aeons it took for the neocortex to evolve and finally distinguish human beings from all other life forms.

Growing almost as a separate organ atop the midbrain, the neocortex is the organ of humanity. It is the most distinguishing anatomical feature among the higher mammals, as the comparative anatomy of apes, chimpanzees, hogs, and bears graphically shows.

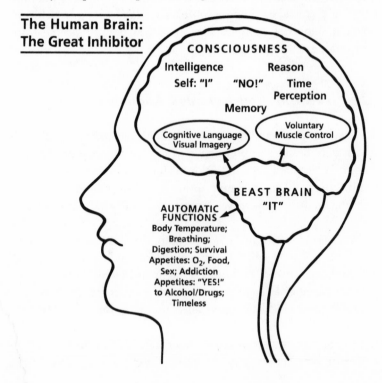

The Human Brain: The Great Inhibitor

CONSCIOUSNESS

Intelligence   Reason

Self: "I"   "NO!"   Time Perception

Memory

Cognitive Language Visual Imagery

Voluntary Muscle Control

BEAST BRAIN "IT"

AUTOMATIC FUNCTIONS
Body Temperature; Breathing; Digestion; Survival Appetites: O_2, Food, Sex; Addiction Appetites: "YES!" to Alcohol/Drugs; Timeless

It is the organ of human thought, of intelligence, of reason, of language, of inhibition. It is probably the most sophisticated organization of matter in the universe.

One's midbrain recognizes internal cues for action that will help it survive. For example, one may feel hunger while walking the aisles of a market, and the midbrain will recognize the plentiful food. When the display of fresh strawberries comes into view, one may suddenly have a plan of action to take a strawberry and eat it on the spot. Along with this plan or idea of eating the berry, one may feel a strong appetite for eating it, as well as a sense of being drawn to pick it up and bite into it. Were it not for the inhibitory function of the neocortex, which is responsible for voluntary actions, intelligence, reasoning, and delay of gratification, open displays of food in markets would be quite impossible. People would simply do what comes naturally and help themselves to what they desire. In other words, civilization depends largely on neocortical functioning to inhibit impulses for immediate gratification. When the midbrain says, "Yes, do it now!" the neocortex, understanding the larger context of the behavior says, "No, not now. At least pay the cashier first." Other states of arousal, including sex, follow the same pattern of midbrain arousal and neocortical inhibition, at least for most people. For this good fortune, we enjoy some degree of civilization.

But in some people a strange anomaly develops, wherein one's ability to inhibit the desire to eat food becomes impaired. Whether this anomaly is a disease, or an inherited talent, an inherited appetite, psychological condition, a personality trait, an astrological outcome, or is simply a condition sparked by periods of pleasurable overeating seems less important than to recognize that there is a pathological relationship between the midbrain and the neocortex. The midbrain has come to a commanding position of authority in deciding when to eat and how much to eat. This difficulty is compounded by the gustatory experience, which some people describe as "orgasmic" and which leads people to eat with wild abandon.

Addictive Voice Recognition Technique (AVRT) includes awareness of not only the conscious thoughts and images that support overeating but also an appreciation of where, in the structures of the brain, they may be referenced. When one is experiencing the desire to overeat, it is essential not only to recognize the idea itself as against one's self-interest, but also to recognize its biological source. To understand that the desire to overeat is emanating from an organ that is on a par with a dog's brain is quite helpful in understanding it and assigning it an appropriate degree of credibility.

AVRT is based on an understanding that the brain consists of *two separate organs,* the midbrain and the neocortex, each communicating with the other. The midbrain enlists the functions of the neocortex in the consummation of appetites. A cognition "I want a doughnut" originates in the midbrain and is an expression of an appetite that has enlisted the language functions of the neocortex. But the neocortex, with its adaptive (intelligent) functions, may recognize and inhibit that cognition and, with time, inhibit the appetite itself. When one has a plan to eat correctly, especially a Big Plan for permanent moderation of food intake, it becomes relatively easy to identify *any* food-specific thought, in language or in images, as being against the self-preserving Big Plan—*and therefore an enemy.* To go even farther and identify that cognition as short-range hedonism of the primitive midbrain, and the idea of eating correctly as the long-range hedonism that is made possible by the inhibiting function of the neocortex, help draw out a better understanding of the phenomenological nature of addiction itself.

When the possibility of bingeing is threatened, a wide spectrum of emotions may emerge, including anxiety, anger, panic, and tearful grieving. The most direct threat to the supply, as understood by the subcortical Beast, is by the neocortex, which has the ultimate capacity to deny even the most urgent biological drives, including food (fasting to death), and sex (yes, some clergy do adhere to vows of lifetime celibacy). The Beast of RR, therefore, may be said to have feelings, feelings that can be experienced and assigned to a primitive intelligence. Therefore it is often quite difficult to make a neocortical covenant to eat correctly for good, because of the fear that is understood at a subcortical level. The good news is that like most beasts, the Beast of RR understands authority when it is finally exercised. It collapses under neocortical authority. When the Big Plan is finally accomplished, people often report profound relief that the struggle is over, and then look forward to the mop-up operation of identifying the residuals of addictive yearning.

Understanding this simplified structural model of addiction gives the effect, in many people, of seeing a coherent game board for playing aggressively against a life-threatening condition.

This concept also puts gluttonous behavior into an interesting perspective. The expression "party animal" is appropriate enough, and the expression "eating like a hog" takes on a special meaning. But in RR, instead of viewing overeating as a disease process over which we have little control, we tend to look at past bingeing as the result of a state of neocortical laziness, and the act of bingeing as quite *stupid* rather than a symptom of something poorly understood. The structural model also argues even more forcefully for long-term dietary discipline, because we understand that although there clearly is a fine human defense against the urge to binge, it lies within the neocortex. With this understanding, it seems unacceptably risky then to revitalize the subcortical appetite centers by frequent bingeing.

The structural model described here is far from a perfect model of addiction, but clearly the disease model has run a course of destruction by undercutting human competency. Therefore it is time to build a more rational conception of addiction.

If hunger were intolerable,
No one would survive
To starve
To death.

CHAPTER 4

Eating Correctly

At the heart of Rational Recovery from fatness is an easily learned activity that is indispensable to weight control and, for that matter, general health. We will call that activity "eating correctly." The negative definition of eating correctly is "refraining from eating the wrong foods, in excessive amounts, at the wrong times, and at inappropriate places." When even one of these conditions has been met, one is said to be "eating incorrectly" and perpetuating the problem of overweight. The affirmative definition is "eating the correct foods, at the correct times, in correct amounts, and at appropriate places."

In the following discussion remember that "correct" means something different for everyone. Eating is a very personal activity, and it is not for *Taming the Feast Beast* to tell people what they should or should not do. It is also irrational for you, the overeater, to tell yourself that you should or should not eat such and such, or that you should lose weight, or that you shouldn't overeat. Again, eating is a very personal activity, and in RR you will be eating exactly what you choose to eat. *You* will determine what is "correct" for you to lose weight, and *you* will decide if you are eating correctly or incorrectly.

It is very likely that as you become more involved with your Rational Recovery weight reduction and control program you will, from time to time, eat incorrectly. In that regard, RR is like any other weight control program; you will "blow it" from time to time. (This is not inevitable, but only very likely.) In RR, however, you will be able to *cut your losses* (actually, your gains) greatly when a lapse occurs, and very quickly, guiltlessly, and selfishly resume correct eating. As you become more familiar with rational thinking and concepts, you will find you are less perfectionistic, less demanding and punitive toward yourself, less likely to overgeneralize about failures and lapses, and more able to interrupt incorrect eating before more damage is done.

What Is Correct Food?

Correct food is simply a balanced diet of food you like that is not fattening. Just about anything is correct in tiny amounts, but for your purposes it may be better to abstain from concentrated, fatty foods such as ice cream, pastries, candy, snack foods, fried foods, butter, margarine, mayo, dairy products, and fast foods. Eating fat will make you fat. Instead, foods such as meat (poultry and fish are preferable to fatty or red meats), potatoes, vegetables, bread, fruits, green salads, cereals, and other grains will provide nutrition and satisfy your appetite. This is known to virtually everyone and needs no further discussion in this book. By all means obtain books on diet, nutrition, and exercise and read them for further information on what is good for you. Your physician may also have some good advice for you, based on his or her knowledge of your medical history and current state of health.

What Are Correct Amounts?

These are the amounts of food we intellectually know are sufficient to sustain daily energy, health, and nutrition. The human body is well prepared to function on small amounts of food, although it may sound the starvation alarm (hunger) when usual amounts are reduced. One way to estimate correct amounts of food is to recall the last time you decided not to return to a restaurant because the portions were too small. That was probably the correct amount of food. Meat portions need not exceed four ounces (the size of a Burger King Quarter Pounder patty *after* being cooked), and other servings of veggies and potatoes need not exceed one serving spoon full. A spaghetti dinner can be enjoyed with only half the plate covered and only enough sauce to color the pasta. You will find many ways to eat the food you like in smaller portions, while avoiding persistent hunger between meals. But don't forget, it is quite all right to feel a little hungry and not eat. If you suspect you have a medical condition that requires avoiding states of hunger, consult with your doctor. But if you do not consult with a physician, be wary of your suspicions of a medical condition as an excuse to avoid hunger. Your Feast Beast will lunge at this kind of thinking to get you to eat incorrectly.

Many dieters report that switching to smaller plates, or using a large saucer, is a fine way to reduce one's portions, but one would also have to wonder from a rational viewpoint why it would be so threatening for one actually to see areas on a normal-sized plate uncovered by food. While attempting to lose weight, there is never any justification for having seconds on anything, even if it means going away from the table half hungry. (As you read this, you may notice a sensation of anxiety arising in the pit of your stomach; that uneasy feeling is caused by the stirrings of your Feast Beast as it senses that it may be in for a severe cutback on what it demands from you—a continuous supply of fattening foods, in unlimited quantities. It knows that your overeating is possible only because you are uninformed about correct eating, and it is frightened that with this new information you will soon become its master. It will feel like it is dying, and may struggle explosively against you.) Your physical appetite is regulated in part by recent trends in your food intake, so when you have left the table half hungry for a day or so and not eaten between meals, you will invariably find that your physical appetite is for less food. Diet pop or water helps take the edge off hunger, but in RR you will become much more tolerant of hunger than ever before. Hunger will become your occasional friend, and you will cultivate a new relationship with it. Accordingly, you will eat considerably less food.

What Is the Correct Time to Eat?

Anytime, your Feast Beast would like you to believe, but in a rational context mealtime is the correct time to eat. Some successful dieters report that it is possible to chase away hunger by eating six small meals a day, but one also must wonder why hunger must be chased away at all. Is hunger such a terrible thing? The Feast Beast, which occupies a portion of your mind, thinks that hunger is a terrible thing. What do you think? Is it really *terrible*? Really?

Three modest, balanced meals a day will meet all of your requirements for energy and health, and your body will quickly adapt to that pattern of correct eating. If, after reading all the diet books that insist that breakfast is the most important meal of the day, you could care less for breakfast, then do it your way and skip breakfast. At lunch, though, have a plan for what you will eat, and don't exceed that. If you're a burger or hot dog fan, have one. One! Then get back to work and forget about the second one you wanted. Eat at regular times, two or three times a day, and get on with life. There's so much more to life than eating. Isn't there?

What Are Correct Places to Eat?

Make rules for yourself on where you will do your eating, and stick to them. Typical rules are: Eat at a table at mealtime, in a restaurant, at a picnic, at your desk if you don't go out to lunch, or anywhere usual. But the living room, the bathroom, the car, or while walking down the street, watching TV, playing cards, at your desk while on duty, in bed, on horseback, or other incongruous places are incorrect places to eat food. If you are eating in an incorrect place you are also very likely eating an incorrect food in incorrect amounts at an incorrect time. So knock it off and resume eating correctly.

Getting Down to Business

By adhering to the above parameters or guidelines, you can be fairly certain about whether an eating plan is correct for you. But, you ask, how can I *stick* to these rules?

That's a fair question, and here are some answers.

First, you had better get used to the idea, once and for all, that you *will* become hungry every day for the rest of your life, and during the time you are losing weight you may be more hungry, and hungry more frequently. As a compulsive overeater you have routinely conceded victory to every twinge of hunger and to every urging of the Feast Beast.

In RR, you will be learning to reinterpret the experience of hunger and literally to learn to accept it as a natural, harmless, and —get this—*desirable* feeling.

Let us explain by using the ABC process of rational-emotive behavior therapy.

Let's say that one morning you are occupied in some solitary activity in your home. Suddenly, at 10:30 A.M., your mind drifts from your work and you are acutely aware of a gnawing, empty sensation in your midsection. That is your Activating event.

Then you jump up and grab a cracker from the cupboard. You spread some cheese on the cracker and eat it. That is the Consequence that follows A. You were hungry and then you ate the cracker with cheese. Then you feel guilty because you ate before lunch—a no-no. So you have several more.

It would seem that your hunger caused you to eat and you are unable to control your impulse to eat. Not so in Rational Recovery.

A never causes C because that would require magic. C is only a feeling, and one must do considerable *thinking* about what to do about the twinge of hunger before anything is eaten.

"Oh, no," you may say, "I didn't really *think* about eating. I just felt hungry, and before I could get my bearings, there I was putting cheese on the cracker and then I just kind of automatically popped it into my mouth. Only *then* did I start thinking, when I realized what I had just done, and by then I realized it was too late. So I figured, 'What's the use?' and had a few more."

If this is how it seems, you are not lying or even stretching the truth. You are simply, just like millions of others who eat incorrectly, unaware of some very real thinking and decision-making that always precedes incorrect eating. In the ABC model, B stands for the beliefs that one has about A, and here is where RR comes in, strong and decisive.

When you felt hungry, you immediately began talking to yourself, as described in Chapter 3, "Voices and Visions." You know best what your thought sentences at point B (Beast beliefs) were, but they probably went something like this:

Beliefs: Oh-oh. I'm hungry. I *need* something to eat. But it's only ten-thirty. But I've *got* to have something. I feel miserable. I can't *stand* this feeling. I can't put up with it. What is there? Something little. Anything. Soup. No. Too much trouble. Just something little. Quick. A nibble. Ah! Crackers! Yes! Where are they? On the counter. No. The cupboard. There they are. Ugh. Dry. Put something good on them. What? Cheese spread! Where is it? Fridge. There it is. Still good? Yep, most of it. Knife. There. Now see if it's good. Hmmm . . . not bad. That'll hold me till lunch.

You see, there is *lots* of thinking here, and the decision to eat was very consciously made. The idea that one is *mysteriously* driven to eat irresponsibly is an *illusion* that is perpetuated by overeaters themselves. Some dependency programs for overeaters even require members to confess that they are powerless over their impulses to eat incorrectly and therefore must rely on something other than or greater than themselves to eat correctly. From a rational viewpoint, that is about the *worst thing* to tell someone who is already having trouble with impulse control.

Instead, recall the map of the brain on page 60, and envision the language center in the neocortex as a contested area. Turf. The thinking described above demonstrates that the Feast Beast (subcortical appetite) is using your language faculty to support a food binge.

But let's see what else you may tell yourself after eating the forbidden cracker at ten-thirty in the morning in your home:

Irrational Beliefs: Now look what I've done! And it was just last night that I vowed I wouldn't do this. What a stupid ass I am. Just like always. I'll never be any different. I was going to wait for sure until lunch and then just have a chicken leg with toast and coffee. I broke my promise to myself, and I'm still hungry, dammit. Hell, it's only ten thirty-two. Oh, phooey on it all. What's the use? I'll start over tomorrow. No use even trying today. Down the hatch. Ugh. They don't even taste good. What am I doing? I'll never lose weight. I'm just a permanent fatty. Who cares? At least it's better than not eating.

This line of thought is much easier to recall, because it is after the fact (after the Feast Beast has prevailed) and also because the pain of hopelessness, defeat, and guilt stands out clearly in your memory. Thus it seems in retrospect that you started thinking only after the fact, as you hypothetically stated above. In reality, *you were in total control of yourself the entire time,* and eating the crackers was the result of a *decision* you made to eat crackers.

You can certainly learn to make better decisions if that's what you want, and RR is an ideal instrument for achieving that goal. Fortunately, your decisions to eat improperly are based on sloppy, crooked thinking, and you are provided here with the means to sharpen your thinking when you are hungry. Below is a full illustration of Rational Recovery from imminent relapse, using the ABC model, this time including D and E, as you will be doing from here on.

Activating event: I feel hungry, empty inside.

Beliefs about A: I'm hungry. I *need* something to eat. I feel *miserable.* I *can't stand* this feeling, and I've *got* to have something. I *can't put up* with this empty feeling any longer. What is there?

Something little. Anything. There are some crackers. Not much, but I will eat them right now.

Consequence: I ate crackers with cheese before lunch.

New Activating event: I ate crackers with cheese before lunch.

Beliefs: Now look what I've done! I broke my promise to myself, and I'm still hungry, dammit. What a stupid ass I am. Just like always. I'll never be any different. Oh, phooey on it all. What's the use? I'll start over tomorrow. No use even trying today. I'll never lose weight. I'm just a permanent fatty. Who cares? At least it's better than not eating.

Consequence: I felt guilty, hopeless, ashamed, worthless, *and I ate even more crackers and cheese!*

Disputing B$_1$: If I'm hungry, does that mean I *need* to eat something now? Or do I merely want to eat something? *Must* I eat right now, really? Of course I don't absolutely have to eat right now. I wouldn't die for over a month if I started a total fast right now. Is this feeling of hunger really miserable? Is this feeling of emptiness *intolerable,* so that I *can't stand it*? If I can't stand this feeling, then what am I doing right now? I'm standing it! And I'm not miserable in the least. I'm just a tad hungry, that's all! Why can't I just be hungry for a few hours? Am I an infant who can't wait for the bottle? Am I really so deficient that I can't be hungry for a few minutes or even a few hours? Of course not. Being hungry is what I've been waiting for, because that means I'm using up my fat reserve. Therefore, I'll choose to *value* my hunger feelings instead of hating them. I can desire hunger the same way athletes desire fatigue. No pain—no gain, only here it's no pain—no loss. To destroy a pleasant hunger once I've worked all day to develop it is stupid, so I'll *cultivate* my present hunger and make it last until my next scheduled meal. And that's that!

Effect (emotional): I felt much more comfortable even though I was still hungry.

Effect (behavioral): I got back to work and forgot about the empty feeling.

Disputing B₂: If I have failed to eat properly, does that make me a stupid ass? Well, not really. It only proves that I'm imperfect and not that I'm a stupid, worthless, or blameworthy person. If I've had this trouble for a long time, does that mean I can never get better? Hardly, for now I'm on the track of something that makes sense and I can see how I will change myself for the better. There is no evidence that I can't lose weight, even though I've always been heavy. Who cares that I had a cracker? I do, because it's my life, and I want to enjoy myself as much as I can, and losing weight is one way I can get more pleasure for myself. I certainly do care about losing weight, even though I just had a slip and ate a few crackers with cheese. Now I'll get right on with what I was doing and have no more of this silliness about having myself an extended food binge just because I feel hungry. Besides, I *want* to feel hungry! How else can I ever burn off my fat reserve unless I feel some hunger? I can't, so I'll learn to *cultivate* the hungry feeling and *appreciate* it.

Effect (emotional): I felt guiltless about eating incorrectly and found my hunger far less compelling.

Effect (behavioral): I avoided a serious weight loss relapse and returned to productive activity.

Rational Recovery is a process of reasoning that leads to a desired goal, but eventually it becomes second nature to think clearly in difficult situations. RR changes in a relatively short time from a self-conscious effort to analyze thoughts and feelings into an *attitude* of confidence and self-control. The ABC's shown above are an example of how you can begin to work on your own pattern of overeating, and it is recommended that you sit down when you are tempted to eat incorrectly and write down your own experience. There is something special and therapeutic about writing down your thoughts at times of conflict. First, it forces you to formulate your ideas clearly, and second, you are then able to see at a glance the merits of various ideas you have written.

Some folks are highly resistant to doing any writing exercises, and it is this writer's hunch that Mr. Feast Beast is telling those individuals such things as, "Oh, to hell with it. It won't really do anything, and you'll just feel awkward and stupid. You can figure things out in your head, silly." Your Feast Beast is highly opposed to any serious progress on dietary discipline, and will sabotage your efforts to gain control of your eating behavior all along the way. So do it. Sit down when you are tempted to have a tiny binge, and start writing. Keep a sheet of paper and a pen near the refrigerator, and when you start foraging for something at the wrong time, grab the pen instead of a cold cut. Do some ABC's on paper if possible, or, very briefly, you can identify the probable irrational idea and dispute it in your head. For example, the central idea of this impulse to eat may be, "I need something to eat." Ask first, "Is there any evidence that I need something right now?" Then ask, "Is there any evidence that I don't need it?" Ask a good question, get a good answer.

Running on Empty

It might be helpful to think of the fuel gauge in your automobile when you feel hungry. Remember that you can go many miles "running on empty." The car runs just as well as on a full tank, but, of course, it is necessary to fuel up from time to time. Note that the expression used here is "fuel up" instead of "fill up."

"Running on empty" is a way of summing up a weight loss attitude that allows you to understand what you are really doing to yourself when you are losing weight. You are limiting your fuel intake so that your fuel reserves are consumed, or converted to energy. When you find yourself feeling sorry for yourself because you feel "empty," a rational antidote is simply to remind yourself that you are now doing what you chose earlier to do, which is running on empty. Biologically, we are very well prepared to run on empty for long periods of time, unless there is some medical condition such as diabetes or hypoglycemia. That is why it is advisable to consult with a physician as part of your plan to lose weight, especially if you suspect that you aren't in good physical condition.

When you run on empty for a time—say, a week or so—you will probably notice that you think less and less about food. There may even be a tendency to forget meals, because running on empty leaves you with the energy and freedom to become involved in other fascinating activities.

Some people report that they seem to have a little more energy while running on empty. One possible explanation for this is that our nomadic ancestors may have had to travel long distances to obtain food, and they literally "ran on empty" to survive. It is well known that hunger triggers increased physical activity in most creatures, large and small. When you next find yourself feeling restless and foraging in the refrigerator, remind yourself that your ancient ancestors used this restlessness to travel hundreds of miles on foot between meals. Surely you can make it until dinnertime.

The Feast Beast Goes Shopping

You may have noticed that if you go to the grocery store while you are running on empty, you may end up with more purchases than you originally intended. Grocery shopping, very clearly, is a bingeing opportunity, and a trip to the store can be classified as a food binge when incorrect foods are purchased. You are probably aware of various feelings as you walk in the aisles, picking and choosing among the amazing variety of foodstuffs. You may feel hurried at times, wanting to check out, or annoyed at unsupervised children who scream or who play with the merchandise. But you may also notice the sense of pleasure as you contemplate choice foods. At these times, especially when you are hungry, your Feast Beast is at its best. It will find ingenious ways to persuade you to cart home large amounts of concentrated foods such as snacks, pastries, ice cream, thick steaks, cookies, dairy products, and much, much more.

Sometimes the Feast Beast will tell you that an item is for others and not for you—"This will be just for company (the children, spouse, etc.)." Of course, the item in question just happens to be something you personally drool over.

Another Feast Beast tactic is to persuade you that you should stock up on something to save time and money later—"It's on sale; I really shouldn't pass this up," or "I'll stock up on lots of bagels and cream cheese because I hate to come to the store so often." Of course, these items are perishable and not the kinds of food that store well, including fresh vegetables, breads, bakery goods, fruits, and so forth. When you have too much on hand, menus tend to get overly developed and meals turn into buffets.

But the most common Feast Beast ploy is simply, "Oh, why not? I can make this last for a long time by just having a little at a time." Regardless of what kinds of reasons you find for incorrect shopping, Rational Recovery provides you an excellent means to stay on course.

Sometimes it may seem as though you are not really thinking as you make unwise food purchases, but, of course, you are. To check your impulses in the aisles and avoid shopper's self-defeat, you may try the following approach. In the parking lot, before you enter the store, tell your Feast Beast that you are aware of it, and you will be waiting to see what it has to say once you are inside. If you have a shopping list, make sure it is in keeping with your rational self-interest, and then tell your Feast Beast that it may as well not even try to get you to stray from the list. Then, as you travel through the aisles, listen carefully for your own ideas of bingeing or incorrect eating. Be alert for mental images of feasting on delicious foods, and when they occur, recognize that you are witnessing the enemy that has been hidden in your consciousness for all those years of overshopping and overeating. Now you are finally in a position to gain the advantage over one of your own most personal patterns of self-defeat.

On "No-Hunger Plans"

Many diet books boast that by eating certain foods, according to their plans, you may avoid hunger and still lose weight. For example, "eat only when hungry" works fine for some people, while "eat a little bit frequently" works better for others, as long as either approach avoids fatty foods. Rational Recovery advises you to research these claims yourself by reading and following any of those plans if avoiding hunger is truly important to you. After all, it is better if you don't have to contend with hunger. However, now that you have *Taming the Feast Beast*, you will be much better prepared to *accept* whatever feelings of hunger you still may have, even though you are following a no-hunger plan to a tee.

"Dieters" often come to resent the imposed structure and discipline contained in detailed eating plans of any kind. With the improvements in the areas of frustration tolerance and impulse control that come from reading this book, those independent souls may be better prepared to achieve and maintain a desired weight with a minimum of structure. Simply eating less of everything and eating at longer intervals (eating correctly) will achieve the usual goals for most overweight persons.

The human body is quite adaptable, and with time and perseverance one may break through the "hunger barrier." Along with correct eating, one may use many helpful techniques, such as drinking lots of water, exercising, and eating smaller meals more frequently.

Don't read this chapter. AVRT is stupid.
—your Feast Beast

CHAPTER 5

AVRT and Your Big Plan

The Feast Beast Plans for the Future

The concept of "going on a diet" is a seed of self-defeat, because it implies its opposite, which is "going *off* a diet." Remember that the Feast Beast is quite adept at protecting the supply of desirable food and that the midbrain, the site of the appetite for food, is quite adept at getting what it wants. For millions of years, primitive human beings (running on the "old brain," or midbrain) withstood harsh environmental challenges to survival, including famine, and the fittest ones among them could sense the location of food, compete for it, pursue and seize it, eat it, and store the rest in caches or as body fat for later use. Only the ones who mastered these talents survived to pass them on to their offspring. Body fat has always, until recent history, had high survival value. Even in the past few centuries, body fat was a sign of affluence and social status, and even an element of sexual attractiveness and beauty.

Your Feast Beast has an uncanny, even *ruthless,* intent to survive by sensing the location of food, obtaining it, making it taste good, eating it, and preserving the future supply of it, either in raw form or as adipose tissue. In other words, *it wants you to get fat,* to endure (self-imposed) famine, so it can fatten you once again. Almost invariably, dieters seem eagerly to look forward to the end of the diet. Indeed, for the Feast Beast it is either feast or famine.

One might say that your midbrain *resents* your neocortex (which is "you"), and when you cheat your midbrain of what it demands, it will first rebel, by telling you how awful it is to be deprived of "all you want." Then, if you insist on not satisfying your hunger, it will patiently wait until a better feasting opportunity is present later—when the diet/famine is over.

If your goal is to lose weight and keep it off, then you had better confront this reality forthrightly, by deciding about the roles of food and hunger in your life. These decisions are based on your intelligence, which is very clearly a function of your neocortex. Now that you are *intellectually* aware of the origins of your endless struggle against cyclical weight gain, you can recognize your persistent, addictive voice as a voice from your distant, ancestral past—a voice from the jungle urging you to eat far more than is good for you, and more than is necessary for immediate survival.

Yes, the questions of whether to live to eat, or eat to live are before you. And be assured that you can decide to reverse an earlier decision that you will live to eat. You may not recall deciding to be fat, but the decision was made once in your earlier years, then again, and then again and again. You have made the decision to be fat every day for many years, even though it seems that you are a victim of unknown circumstances. The decision to be fat is embedded in your intellectual passivity toward hunger itself, and the quiet voice that seduces you to eat excessively and incorrectly. In the ABC exercises described in Chapter 4, "Eating Correctly," and in the ones later in the book, the irrational ideas that support your bingeing are the enemies of your health and happiness, so your work, very clearly, is aggressively to dispute—yes, attack—those beliefs with your best neocortical intelligence. While this may be difficult at first, there is some good news to come.

But It's Only a Beast

Although your subcortical Feast Beast is remarkably efficient in its food-seeking tactics, it is no match for the remarkable neocortex that is "you." Like most beasts, your Feast Beast understands authority. If you have ever been followed by a growling dog, you may have been aware that your options were either to keep walking at the same pace; start running; or, quite decisively, turn on the dog and face it down. Most often, the canine beast will cut and run when faced by an advancing human many times its own size. There is a clear pecking order throughout the animal kingdom, where the larger or smarter creatures dominate the smaller or dumber ones. Your neocortex is not only many times larger than your midbrain, but also the most sophisticated entity in the known universe. It can master both its physical and psychological environments, and quite readily, *given the correct coded information,* suppress *any* appetite and defeat *any* addiction. Political activists often fast themselves to death for higher values than food, drug addicts stop using drugs through their own free will, and others enter lifelong celibate states as a means to obtain higher priorities and fulfillments.

The Big Plan for Dietary Discipline vs. One Day at a Time

In RR, you are provided a means for moment-to-moment dietary discipline in the Addictive Voice Recognition Technique (AVRT) and in the ABC approach for avoiding emotional pitfalls that can make this discipline difficult. Rational living is an elegant life-style that presents human happiness as a high ideal. But because of the persistence of the addictive voice, the so-called Feast Beast, strong and decisive measures are quite appropriate and useful.

In the above discussion of feast and famine, we learned that there is an appetite in the inner brain for unlimited food, forever. While many people believe that weight control is better done "one day at a time," RR presents a revolutionary concept of deciding, once and for all, to eat correctly. In what some call the "Big Plan," the decision is made to eat correctly, forever.

How to Make Your Big Plan for Eating Correctly

In the earlier discussion of Addictive Voice Recognition, you learned about the structural model of addiction, along with some introduction of the Feast Beast concept/device. Here we will go much farther, by exploring the process of AVRT along with the buildup to establishing permanent change in your attitude toward food and eating, even before you begin to change your eating habits. In the following paragraphs you will learn the rules of the game.

First, it is extremely important for you to understand that a Big Plan is entirely unnecessary. So is losing weight, if you recall. To think that you must have a Big Plan to lose weight is not only inaccurate, but by musturbating this way you will also sow the seeds of failure. Second, you may certainly lose weight on an open-ended basis, and at any time you choose, implement your Big Plan. Third, a Big Plan is irreversible. That is why many people choose not to commit themselves to a Big Plan. They say, "I like to keep my options open. Never say 'never.' " And this is fine. The Big Plan is *major* decision-making, and one had better give serious thought to a covenant that will remain in effect until death. If you are actively considering a Big Plan for yourself after reading only this far, stop. Think. Be careful. Read on before any further commitment. A Big Plan may not be for you at all. You may do much better with sporadic dietary discipline.

The Key

Now, the first question you will ask yourself is, "What is my *present* plan for future overeating?" Ah, yes. This *is* the question, now, isn't it?

If by now you are grinning or chuckling, you have gotten the entire point of AVRT, the Feast Beast, and the Big Plan—all at once. If you are feeling a little uneasy, ditto. If you feel like slamming this book down, or sending to the publisher for a refund of the money you paid for this silly trash, ditto. If you feel tearful, and have a tear on your cheek, it's all the same as the grin, the anxiety, the anger, the sadness. Your Feast Beast has feelings! Strong feelings!

What is your real plan for overeating? Are you going to do it anymore? Eating is always a choice, isn't it? *Isn't it?*

Of course it is, and no matter how many diets you've been on, how many programs you've tried, drugs you've tried, and no matter how long you've been struggling with your weight, you have always *chosen* to resume eating the wrong foods, in extra amounts, at the wrong time, in the wrong places.

Think back to the last time you "broke your diet." Maybe it was a candy bar in the car on a trip to the shore, a triple burger instead of grilled cheese, a milkshake instead of a diet soda, or whatever. Who *was* it who chomped down on that forbidden morsel? Was it Tallulah Bankhead? Jimmy Carter? No, it was you. And you also tasted it, swallowed it, digested it, and shat it out the next day, slightly fatter, of course, for your mistake.

Yet you *still* intend to overeat *any old time you feel like it*! You may diet here, there, diet now and diet later, long diets, short diets, experimental diets, and serious diets.

As promised throughout *Taming the Feast Beast*, you are being challenged here and now to take responsibility for your eating behavior. There are two parts of this responsibility: your past overeating and your future overeating. If you are having any difficulty accepting full responsibility for every ounce of your body fat, here are some questions to clarify:

- Can you eat a lot of food without being aware of eating the food?
- Can you overeat without being aware that you are eating incorrectly?
- Does fat tissue come from nothing? Where does the body fat come from? The air? Water? A virus?
- Do you really believe that your overweight is caused by something other than eating too much food?
- When you serve yourself food, do you make sure you get enough? Enough for what?

- Do you become irritated when restaurant portions are modest?
- Are you more likely to overeat while alone?

These and other good questions are important to ask yourself so you may recognize that overeating is a behavioral disorder. There is simply no way to maintain your overweight condition without providing the necessary amount of nutrition, and no way to gain weight without consuming more energy than your activities consume. (Fluid retention doesn't count as weight gain.)

Now, if you are clear about the connection between your decisions to overeat and your overweight, you are ready for the next question:

How do you feel (the emotion) about significantly reducing your intake of food for the rest of your life? Or, to put it more bluntly, how do you *feel* about never overeating again?

If you aren't sure about this question, here is a clarifying procedure:

Think about the entire rest of your life, and all the possible situations in which you are likely to want to overeat. This includes when you are bored, depressed, happy, having fun, alone, with people, at funerals, at weddings, among relatives and family, on picnics, at home with family, at home alone, when you are very hungry, when you are exposed to delicious free food at a party, when you are in an expensive restaurant, when you are at a smorgasbord, when your favorite food is served by your host in her home, at Thanksgiving, after a long hike, when you are older, when you are driving alone, or at any other time you can think of when it would seem fine really to dig into the chow.

Once again, now, *think* of never eating more than a single serving—one that looks too small—only at regular mealtimes, for the rest of your life. *Add* to this, eliminating forever your favorite food (ice cream, lobster, steak, Chinese food, you name it). How does it feel?

It is very likely an unpleasant feeling. It may be sadness, anxiety, depression, anger, or another bad feeling. Listen to your thoughts about this deprivation, too. Write them down.

The feeling that this exercise produces *is* your Feast Beast. You are feeling your addiction to food, your personal nemesis, your personal enemy itself, the Feast Beast of Rational Recovery. The thoughts you hear are the *sounds* of your Feast Beast. "That would be terrible," it may say. "You can't do it. It (weight loss) isn't worth it," you may hear. "Put this book down," it may urge.

But, somewhere high in your neocortex, that part of the brain that is reading this material, is another voice, the voice of you. That voice may be saying, "Yes, this is the truth of the matter, the problem I've had all along. I *have* been quite passive toward my appetite for food, and I yield to it and then make up all kinds of excuses about how all of my siblings are fat and so was my mother, and my metabolism is slower than that of normal people, and I had such a rotten childhood, and my mother fed me too much, and food is a substitute for love, and I ain't gettin' enough love, so I eat. And much worse, I don't even *plan* to give up on overeating because I love to eat too much." That is your intelligence at work. RR is a plan for dietary discipline based on human intellect.

If your discomfort with an experimental Big Plan is obvious to you, and you can hear your disturbing thoughts about correct eating, then you are recognizing your addictive voice. Already you are getting the hang of Addictive Voice Recognition Technique (AVRT).

The next phase is to recognize this feeling as your enemy. Simple, but not so easy at first. After all, the feelings are quite real, and *convincing*. When you think of how pleasurable eating is, it is sad to think of never really diving into the grub again. And it *isn't* fair that life offers so few simple, predictable pleasures, and most people can eat whatever they want and you can't get away with it. And what *will* it be like, at those special times when it will be so enticing to go ahead and binge on something really, really good? It will be sooooo painful to look at the forbidden food, droooooling, craving, desiring, almost tasting all that wonderful foooood. How awful to turn away unsatisfied. Worse than coitus interruptus. And how *will* you get through bad times when food has always been there to take the edge off? How dreadful.

But these are the very ideas that comprise the philosophy of fatness, and you are already, in previous pages here, actively learning to dispute them in your neocortex so that you may send an authoritative, rational message inward to your subcortical Feast Beast, saying, in effect, "No!" At some point it may come to your awareness that any thinking that supports any overeating, ever, is of the Feast Beast and therefore against your interests. At that point you have made a transition from active disputing to automatic refusal of extra food. When you have learned to recognize your Feast Beast voice and dispute it *in vivo*—that is, as you drive past the bakery shop; as you pass the refrigerator; while you are cooking; while you are watching TV; and, most importantly, while you are eating correctly—you may be ready to institute a Big Plan.

Beast Recognition and the Mental Faculties

People who compulsively overeat in spite of great distress over the consequences may be said to be "all Beast." They are simply uninformed about the mechanism for dietary discipline. They are unable to recognize the cognitive antecedents of their eating behavior so that they may decide otherwise. It seems to them that they have no choice but to eat unwisely and that they are powerless to do otherwise. The addictive voice—the Beast—has gained control of one or more mental faculties.

For example, let's take Bill, who is unhappy about gaining weight even though he eats large chocolate sundaes every night. To discourage his impulsive indulgences, he empties his freezer of ice cream, but then he goes out to an ice cream parlor after the news each evening and has his "hit" of ice cream. Although he sincerely plans to stop his self-destructive habit, he changes his mind each evening and runs out for an ice cream fix. "Something just comes over me," he laments, "and I get up from the TV, and the next thing I know I'm at the parlor with a sundae in front of me. I eat it reading a newspaper, and then on the way home I feel like an idiot for doing something that is ruining my sex life. I make a plan to stop it, but then I hear this voice in my head that says, 'We'll see.' "

If Bill is pressed to explain what "comes over" him, he explains, "Well, when the news is over, it's seven o'clock, and I think, 'What's there to do?' Then I hear myself think, 'Let's go for it.' I get a picture of the parlor and the sundae in my head, and I'm on my feet and going for my car keys."

How does Bill feel when he is mobilizing for the fix? "Weird," he says. "Like I know this is stupid, but who gives a shit? There's nothing to do, and I know I really like to eat a hot fudge sundae at the parlor while reading the paper. So I think, 'We need a little treatie-poo.'"

Does Bill have any second thoughts before leaving for the parlor? You bet. "I think, 'You won't do this tomorrow night. Let's get moving.' So off I go, kind of blank-minded."

Faculties and Pronouns

Bill's Beast has gained control of his language and his motor faculties. These are two important functions within the neocortex. People with brain damage from strokes or head injury very often have paralysis of the extremities and difficulty understanding or expressing language, symbolic or verbal. When the language centers of the neocortex are "under the influence" of the midbrain's appetite centers, goal-directed words and sentences become conscious. Goal-(food)-oriented imagery is "seen" in the mind's eye, and finally the motor centers respond to the language and imagery we call the addictive voice, or the Beast. Quite literally, Bill is not in control of his faculties at seven each evening. But his Beast certainly is. His recovery from compulsive overeating depends on his neocortex (Bill) regaining control over his faculties.

And here is how it is done in RR. Bill's intelligence shows him that he is behaving stupidly, and he quite reasonably removes a convenient supply of ice cream from his home. But his Beast reaches out and grasps at his reasoning faculty and "reasons" that he will soon stop bingeing anyhow, and that he can't tolerate boredom, and that he deserves a midevening treat. But Beasts are invariably stupid, because they always want only "that one thing" and because they expose themselves to recognition by the use of certain pronouns.

Notice that at the time of greatest conflict about going out to the parlor, Bill, *who was alone at home,* was thinking, "You won't do this tomorrow night. Let's get moving."

Now, this is pretty strange. Who is this other party, speaking in the second person, "You"? What's this "let's" business? *Let's* get moving? *We* need a little treatie-poo?

This all begins to make sense when we recall the structural model of addiction wherein the "brain" consists of *two organs speaking to each other.* That's right. The midbrain, by seizing the language faculty, is able to make its demands known through conscious thought, and the neocortex, almost a separate entity, speaks for itself through the same language centers. Consequently, addicted people are ambivalent about their substance abuse and have internal, conflicted dialogue about their substance of choice. When we understand that the midbrain will do anything to satisfy itself, and plays by no rules of ethics or morality, it becomes apparent that it is quite capable of using subverted logic and using subverted language to get what it wants: ice cream. So it will address the neocortex as "you" when it is explaining why it is a good idea to indulge, and will use the pronouns "let's" and "we" when it is being impatient and highly persuasive, to speak for both parties at once in a highly effective, seductive way. "We need a little treatie-poo" is a perfect example of this innocent, seductive quality that characterizes some Beast talk. If you will listen to your own addictive voice, you may notice plural pronouns used in a highly inappropriate way, along with occasional "you," as in "You can handle just a little this time."

But bright people can play word games in the interest of survival, too. Here is one of the most potent elements of AVRT that you can use any time you are conflicted over food:

Stay in the first person, with the understanding that plural pronouns are not "I." Any time that the pronoun "I" appears in your consciousness in connection with incorrect eating, just add a "t," transforming "I" to "It." "It," of course refers to the Beast. Here is an example from Bill once again: "I really like to eat a hot fudge sundae at the parlor while reading the paper." If he wants to master his addictive voice, he may first of all recognize that he is thinking of eating incorrectly and then change all pronouns to "it." His new insight is: "It—my Beast—really likes to eat a hot fudge sundae at the parlor while I read the paper." By doing this psychological sleight of hand, Bill has not only outfoxed his ice cream Beast but he has also dissociated from the appetite itself, and may very likely feel relief from acute craving sensations. Try this. See for yourself.

But the semantic part of AVRT continues, and the logic is inexorable. Start listening for all pronouns when you are considering food. The only pronoun that is appropriate when making decisions about eating is "I." The other pronouns are "you," "we," and "us." If you hear, "We need a snack," you have heard your Beast. If you hear, "You are doing very well on your diet," that is your Beast setting you up for a binge. "You will never lose weight," obviously, is from the Beast. If you hear, "I will never be able to lose weight," just add the "t" and see the obvious truth.

"I am hungry" becomes "It wants food." Now you may decide how much to give, the same way you would feed a dog in a pen. It will appreciate every morsel and look forward to more, just like a good doggie. It may whine a little, but the good master or mistress knows it won't die and that overweight kills. While you are eating, your Beast may want to ingest the food as a hungry dog does, "wolfing it down." But since you have a human neocortex, you may choose to abide by the rules of etiquette, even though you feel quite hungry.

To say "It wants food," incidentally, is more accurate than to say "I am hungry." There are problems with the state of being words (is, was, were, be, am, been) that trip people up psychologically. "It wants food" is very accurately saying, "It (my body) wants (as experienced in the midbrain) food."

I lose, I gain,
But never
Maintain

CHAPTER 6

Our Unmiraculous Recovery from Fatness

In Rational Recovery, we already know that our "crimes of the palate" are driven by strong, unpleasant feelings, and when we overeat we are simply trying to control those feelings. We have already tried numerous methods to control our food intake, including iron-willed discipline, structured diets, calorie counting, crash diets, fad diets, balanced diets, unbalanced diets, and dependence on others to provide our discipline. We have experimented with various substitute dependencies and we have tried turning our lives over to external authority, but our native intelligence prevents us from taking these approaches seriously. We have sought professional help and medical remedies and come to resent the kindness of those who make any of these sound so simple. We have watched our weight rise and fall and felt the surges of hope and despair that are part of fatness. And we are ashamed that so simple a problem, limiting the food we eat, should escape our control.

In Rational Recovery, we are not struggling to eat less, or to lose weight, or to follow a diet, or to get smaller waists, or to change our physical dimensions. As desirable as those things may be, we no longer struggle at them, because we already know that it doesn't work to struggle against the tide. Instead, we are seeking to correct some irrational ideas that cause and perpetuate overeating and the weight loss relapse cycle. Ours is more an intellectual struggle than an emotional one. The court for our struggle is within the organ of human thought—the brain—where primary concepts clash, and we are the referees, the final judges of what we will believe.

RICHARD

I'm not much at telling about myself, but I'm glad I found out about RRS. All of my life I have been fat, and now I'm down 120 pounds from my recent peak weight of 340 pounds. I'm a truck driver, so there's plenty of time on the road to get all fired up for the next fast food or truck stop. Trouble is, I got to the point that my job was in danger on account of being so heavy that I wouldn't meet some safety standards the company has. Getting into the cab got so hard for me that I had to install extra foot- and handholds. For years and years I have been a forager, thinking about food all the time I'm not busy at something, and feeling like I'm always on the make for something good to eat. Using the ideas in The Small Book: A Revolutionary Alternative for Overcoming Alcohol and Drug Dependence *that I borrowed from a friend, I have finally gotten a handle on my appetite for food. Not that the appetite has gone away; it just isn't getting the best of me anymore. I think the key thing here is getting up the* confidence *when I'm around food.*

I think I tried everything to lose weight, but it seemed my heart wasn't in it. I felt hopeless that I would ever be anything else than fat, and I felt my eating was something I had no power to control. When I discovered my Beast voice, all of a sudden I could resist eating at will, and I can now see that my weight problem is pretty much a thing of the past. Recognizing the Beast is so simple that I had overlooked it, and I think that anyone who goes on a diet is actually using the Beast idea in The Small Book *without realizing it. Here is how I defeated my Feast Beast after reading about the Beast of alcohol dependence.*

In the past, when I was driving down the road, I would think about many things, but as soon as I felt a little empty inside I would think about food. I would watch for the Golden Arches or some other food joint where I could stop the truck; then I would start braking and pull in. Even when I was ordering my food, I would think how stupid and unnecessary eating that food was, but I would do it anyhow. I would eat it fast, swallowing bite after bite as if I hadn't eaten for days. Sometimes I would take bags of food to eat in the cab, so I wouldn't have to stop so often. This would help me get to my destination on time. I would usually stop to get rid of the trash because I was afraid people would see how much I was eating on the road.

When I learned about the Beast, I decided not to carry any food in the cab and to eat only three times a day, to eat only at restaurants, to eat only single portions of food, and to avoid desserts. I started paying attention to my food ideas, especially the visual pictures in my head. Each time I got the picture of food and it wasn't just before mealtime, I said to myself, "Oops! I'm doing it. Right now, I'm thinking about eating. That's the voice they call the Beast. There you are, you son of a bitch. You are the Beast that causes me all the trouble, and I caught you in the act of going for some food at the wrong time. Nice try, but I'll keep driving until exactly noon, and then I'll start looking for a place to stop." The first time I did this, I was amazed. I felt alert, in control over something that had always controlled me, and I wasn't even hungry!

When noon came and I entered the restaurant, though, my trouble with the Beast wasn't over. I looked at the menu and started looking for the items that would most likely have the most food on the plate. It was the "Truckers' Buffet: ALL YOU CAN EAT" for just $4.95. I pictured myself loading down a huge plate with everything and then returning to get the rest I would need to feel really full, peaceful, and good. Then I recognized the Beast again, and this one time I did something I haven't done since then. I walked out of the restaurant and sat in the truck for a few minutes and thought the whole thing over. I knew I wanted to overeat, as if to make up for being deprived since breakfast, and as if I were malnourished while weighing almost four hundred pounds. It seemed as if everything in me was jangling like an alarm that I would die if I didn't have two or three plates of anything immediately. I actually felt like crying, but all of a sudden I started laughing, and I was laughing at my Feast Beast. I thought, "So this *is* how you work your game! You flash pictures of mountains of food, and then make me feel sorry for myself because I am so hungry. You tell me that life is so hard and there are so few pleasures that *eating is the one thing that is dependable to make me feel okay inside. You tell me that I deserve to eat the Truckers' Buffet because I am suffering from all the effects of being overweight. You make life seem dull and meaningless so that all I can think of is eating away my own boredom with myself. Nice try, Beast. Let's see what you come up with the next time. I'm on to your game, and you're in for big trouble." I went into the restaurant again and ordered one hamburger and a cup of coffee. I was so happy with my sense of self-control that I almost forgot to pay my bill of $3.00.*

That was about eighteen months ago, and I've had many binges since then. Every once in a while, I go off the deep end and eat too much, but I have found that even while I am bingeing I can short-circuit the binge so it isn't so damaging to my gradual weight loss. Understanding the Beast concept is one of the most important insights I have ever had, but using the Beast concept is a skill that improves over time with practice. The most interesting thing about this is that eating normally is getting to be second nature. I've gotten very familiar with my Feast Beast, and I've learned to recognize it in an instant and overpower it with my desire to be good to myself. Now I eat less because I believe that I deserve to feel good.

Richard is a California truck driver who is staying in shape. He has changed his way of thinking about food and about himself, and he has lost weight. There is a general philosophy of Rational Recovery that he does not describe, and the remainder of this chapter will examine some central issues in depth. In the following material, pairs of opposite concepts are presented once again, but this time with some discussion and illustrations. As you read, you will probably recognize the vital part these ideas play in your own life. Reading them will help you to perceive the contrast between fatness and rational living. They are derived from the self-help approach of Albert Ellis, Ph.D., who founded the rational-emotive behavior therapy (REBT) school of thought in modern psychology. Once again, as in Chapter 1, notice how your feelings ebb and flow as you read through the rational and irrational ideas.

1. I am powerless over my urges to eat food and therefore not in control of, or responsible for, what I put into my mouth,
  instead of the rational idea that I have considerable voluntary control over my extremities and facial muscles. ·

Fatness is just a philosophy that justifies continuous overeating. Central to the philosophy of fatness is the concept of powerlessness to control one's eating behavior. Our society is quite forgiving of the nutty idea that people are unable to control what is done with their hands and mouths, but then it is quite unforgiving in its attitudes toward those who *accept* the falsehood of powerlessness and become obese. Because powerlessness suggests the need for a rescuing deity and/or the virtuous assistance and indulgence of others who share in the same philosophy of fatness, twelve-step and other dependency programs thrive.

In RR, we find that powerlessness ideas are the *main causes* of overeating and are in no way therapeutic. As we become more rational beings, we assume total responsibility for each calorie that is ingested, for each morsel that is grasped, and for each whining complaint that seems to justify incorrect eating. The muscles of our hearts and other internal organs are certainly beyond our direct, voluntary control, but in a rational context, nothing could clang so loudly on common sense as the concept of powerlessness over the skeletal muscles that guide food into the mouth.

It is true, however, that we may have trouble *deciding* what to do with our extremities and facial muscles when we feel hungry, but that is a far cry from believing that we are powerless over our actions, our feelings, our decisions, or anything else besides hunger itself. And that leads us to the next fruitcake idea in the philosophy of fatness.

2. My painful emotions and cravings for food are often intolerable and therefore must be controlled by eating food,
  instead of the rational idea that some discomfort is a necessary, inevitable, and entirely harmless part of losing weight.

Hunger doesn't kill—starvation does—and you will have plenty of warning before you die from lack of food. Neither do strong emotions injure you or cause you any harm. You are quite capable of having very bad feelings and living on for better times. Bad feelings won't drive you insane, but your feelings do have some bearing on your actions. You tend to act the way you feel, and you feel the way you think. If you honestly believe that hunger is a *terrible, intolerable* feeling that must be immediately ended, then you will actually increase your discomfort, as described more fully in irrational idea 6, as described on pages 99–101.

In RR you will not only learn to *tolerate* hunger but also to *cultivate* it. That's right—the rational, intentional cultivation of hunger. Recovery from fatness is learning a new relationship with your body, one derived from a philosophy that helps you reduce negative emotions, patterns of self-defeat, and helps you proceed toward your own self-defined goals. Remember?

If you have decided that you sincerely want to lose weight and have decided on a proper weight goal, then it will be necessary for you to experience feelings of hunger from time to time. Necessary! There's no realistic way around it. If you have the courage right now to follow reason to its conclusion, you will see that if (1) I want to lose weight and (2) weight loss requires experiencing hunger, then it is inescapable that (3) for me, it is desirable to feel hungry.

"Now, wait a minute," you may say, "that's too clever. I can't learn to like an ugly feeling!"

Why not? And besides, is hunger really ugly? Or are "ugly" and "bad" and "terrible" and "intolerable" simply your present *definitions* of hunger—definitions that make it seem impossible to resist the urge to eat? You know the answer, because you've been hungry all your life, just like everyone else, fat or thin, and we all know that hunger is just that—hunger—and you can make of it what you choose.

"Oh, but my hunger's different! After all, I am a compulsive overeater. My doctor told me so. Overeaters experience hunger in a way much different from normal persons. That's why we're so fat!" you may respond.

Trash. Drivel. Hunger is hunger, and you know it, and anyone can put up with it, no matter how fat or for how long. If people couldn't tolerate hunger, they wouldn't survive long enough to starve to death. Hunger comes in stages, starting with:

- A mild feeling of emptiness; this will last for about an hour.
- Then come some pangs in the midsection. These will last for less than an hour.
- The pangs increase so that one becomes distracted from other activities. If food is eaten, the pangs go away. If no food is eaten, the pangs subside, and then there is . . .
- A period of restlessness; this will last for several hours, perhaps half a day. During this period of restlessness, one may function well at any complex activity, physical or intellectual. Small amounts of food will provide quick energy but will not remove the hunger. If no food is taken, there will follow . . .
- A feeling of weakness, fatigue, light-headedness, and sometimes clamminess; rest is as useful here as food, but you are in no danger unless you are otherwise ill.

These stages of hunger cover a whole day without nutrition. Those who have fasted know that the second day is a little easier, and during the third there is a lifting of hunger and a renewed sense of lightness. Hunger is so very, very harmless and so obviously tolerable, no matter who you are.

We should also note that these "stages of hunger" are not inevitable and do not follow the same pattern every time you haven't eaten for a while. Much "hunger" is triggered by familiar or learned situations, such as time and place. We tend to become hungry at the same time every day, and it seems to require the same kinds and amounts of food to satisfy our "hunger." People who start skipping breakfast soon don't *get* hungry in the morning, and when one changes the time of the lunch break, hunger soon corresponds with that time of day.

Rational Recovery from fatness does not recommend fasting or even suggest it. The stages of hunger above are described only to demonstrate that there is no basis to your long-held notion that hunger is a terrible feeling that must be immediately quelled.

Closely related to the idea that hunger is intolerable are equally irrational, misleading beliefs harbored by overeaters:

- "What I eat must taste very good" (add mayo, butter, sugar, etc.).
- "Because it tastes so good I can't stop eating" (betcha can't have just one).
- "I shouldn't waste what's left" (the human garbage can syndrome).
- "I truly deserve the supreme joy of eating delicious food" (the *kamikaze* gourmet).

In RR you will come to be acutely aware of these and other utterances of the Beast of Binge. They are actual conscious thoughts that you can hear in your head, and they occur just before and during the binge response.

The appetite is primarily a biological mechanism for preventing weight loss, just as cruise control is a mechanism for preventing speed loss. When hazardous conditions are present, the driver overrides the control mechanism as a matter of survival and self-interest. Learning to override your appetite is the very essence of Rational Recovery from fatness. And you are in the driver's seat!

3. To consider myself a worthwhile person, I must have a "present-able" appearance that no one will find unappealing, unattractive, ugly, fat, overweight, homely, or even plain,
instead of the rational idea that while there are clearly some advantages to looking good to others, I am not dependent on the approval or admiration of others for my sense of personal worth (self-respect).

People of modest proportions are undeniably more attractive to the vast majority of opposite sex, even without the pervasive sexist idealism that is rife in our culture. While a woman who resembled the Venus de Milo sculpture would probably not qualify for a *Playboy* centerfold because of her tummy, and body fat was occasionally a status symbol in more recent centuries, there are no times in history when obesity was idealized for either sex. Even the image of the black "big fat mama" of early twentieth-century advertising seems to reflect more of a racist prejudice than reality. It is doubtful that the overweight black women who were depicted in early American advertising actually were happy about their large proportions, and they probably desired to weigh much less. This is just conjecture, of course, but let's face it: Slim, with very few exceptions, is better than fat. Moreover, fat people will almost invariably suffer some degree of social discrimination and may even be discriminated against vocationally. Clothing manufacturers generally discriminate against fatsos by pretending we don't exist or by making large sizes that are unbecoming to our bodies. The military would much rather have low-profile soldiers who can fit through small spaces fighting in the jungles, and insurance firms bet against us. Coaches won't even let us warm a bench. We are appreciated most by grocers, restaurateurs, Corpulent Clothing, Inc., fat doctors, and publishers of diet books. We are written off as the "fat, jolly ones," yet disdained by passing motorists who ask with a gasp, "How *could* he (she) let himself (herself) *get* that way?" We absorb pervasive "fattist" humor conveying that we are morally defective, stupid, insensitive, and ridiculous. And, alas, we usually don't live as long as slimmer folks.

But isn't it a wonderful thing that as adults we do not *need* the respect of others and that we can think lovingly of ourselves even though others may not?

4. Because I am overweight from eating too much, I should moralistically blame and condemn myself. In other words, to gain some self-respect, I must lose weight,

instead of the rational idea that it is *because* I accept and respect myself that I will limit the food I ingest. Guilt and shame are emotions of childhood that I can now abandon. Both fat people and thin people may enjoy unconditional self-worth provided they are willing to assert that worth authoritatively.

When fat people get weighed and a number appears on the scale indicating the number of pounds, it is as if that number is an inverse rating of their personal worth. In other words, as the number increases, one's sense of worth to oneself decreases. "When I see the scale, I feel guilty (depressed, angry, hopeless, etc.)" is a common remark among the fat. Then, when the scale shows a loss, one may feel a corresponding "lift," as if one's emotions just became "lighter."

Are normal-sized people really intrinsically more worthwhile than fat people? According to many heavyweights, this is so, and this kind of thinking is very common in our neuroticizing culture. TV ads show pictures of successful dieters who exclaim, "Now I like myself so much better! If you can't stand yourself any longer, try the Nutrishame Diet Plan!" Others portray the newly slim remarking, "Now I can go out among people without feeling ugly and ashamed. Now I feel confident of myself." Oh, the *shame* of being overweight! In Rational Recovery, you are learning that you need not lose an ounce to consider yourself a worthwhile human being, and that you may feel quite at ease in public even though others may harbor bigoted, fascistic attitudes toward overweight people.

5. It is a dire necessity for adults to be loved, accepted, and approved of,

instead of the rational idea that adults do not have to get what they want, including love, respect, and acceptance. Rejection is just another's opinion of my worth, one with which I may gullibly agree or rationally disagree. I choose to accept or love myself simply because it feels better than to dislike myself. In this matter, mine is the final word.

Fat people often remark, "Eating is how I meet my emotional needs. Food is my special friend." This is a common starting viewpoint, even though it reflects some irrational thinking. By giving serious thought to this issue—applying your intelligence—you may also learn to become *independent* from the loving or accepting opinions of others. When you accomplish this, which need not require much time, you will have made a great stride toward *emotional independence from food*! People who unconditionally like or accept themselves usually feel well and are in a state of mental health that is conducive to eating correctly. If one is prone to moods of worthlessness, guilt, and depression, one is also far more prone to short-range preoccupations such as food bingeing.

The difficulty, of course, lies in the fact that early on, as little kids, we all really *were* dependent on others, and for everything. Biologically speaking, love is a bond that prevents the starvation of infants and little kids. The connection between love and food is clear in this context, and it can easily spill over into adult life in the form of dependence on the acceptance and loving opinions of others. This kind of emotional dependence is common, but nevertheless it is an obstacle to adult happiness. With some effort it can be overcome at practically any age after adolescence. Simply being aware of the problem, as you are becoming here and now, is more than half the battle.

Psychologically speaking, love is the classroom of self-worth wherein one gathers from the loving opinions of the parent that one is, indeed, a worthwhile being. The difficulty here is that very often one's parent is less than clear on the issue of whether the child is essentially worthy, essentially worthless, or somewhere in between. Many, therefore, enter adulthood with serious doubt about whether they are worthy souls or ones who must now set about to prove, through various culturally prescribed means, that they are really worth their daily bread. Few young adults figure out that one's intrinsic, self-declared worth is a matter entirely separate from the opinions that others may have of them, and that everyone can simply like themselves because it feels better than hating themselves and because no one can stop them from doing it.

Most young children are psychologically dependent on the loving opinions of others largely because of their small, undeveloped brains. Children are like "believing machines" who uncritically accept information provided them by adults, especially their parents. Were this not so, Santa Claus would have little popularity. If I confide to a child of four that I am capable of independent flight and that there are pretty wings concealed beneath my blouse, there is a good chance I will be believed. Children do not play with a full deck; considerable gray matter is missing.

The same child will believe that he or she is morally defective, inferior, worthless, unlovable, or ugly if I express those sincere opinions. Those unprovable ideas will then become the foundation of the child's personality; the child has no way of checking them out and no way to establish a more rational truth—that simply being alive is sufficient to infer his or her own worth. That's too deep for little kids to figure out in the face of adult authority.

As the brain fills out neurologically, the capacity for independent thought and reasoning emerges. The stage is set for the child suddenly to "see through" the problem of personal guilt and worthlessness and exclaim, "Eureka! I'm not worthless! That's just my crazy mother's opinion!" But nooooo, we live in a culture that *perpetuates* the nutty ideas of our ancestors, ideas of externally defined, variable, personal worth; the good-kid, bad-kid syndrome; the fears of disapproval; the idea that adults need love for its own sake; and, in effect, a philosophy of perpetual childhood.

When people discover that as adults they no longer need, but only desire, or prefer, to be loved or approved of by others, an important transition takes place—the transition from emotional dependence on the opinions of others to emotional independence based on rational, unconditional self-acceptance. The results in one's social and personal lives are invariably gratifying, and overweight people are finally prepared to take control of their lives and their eating disorders.

6. *I have little control over my feelings and emotions, which are somehow forced on me by others or external events,*

instead of the rational idea that I feel the way I think, and so have enormous control over my emotions, sorrows, and disturbances.

This irrationality, that emotions are caused by events or other people or by one's past, is a major block to further emotional change and personal growth. As such, it also provides you with an unmatched opportunity for a major breakthrough in overcoming your "fatness." Remember, your "fatness" is an inner condition that remains constant while your weight fluctuates. "Fatness," as we speak of it in Rational Recovery, is the rejection of self that underlies the struggle against overweight—fat or thin, year after year, in sickness and in health, and, unless refuted, till death does its part.

Suppose you undress, look in the mirror, and then feel bad. "Seeing my fat rolls makes me feel bad," you might conclude. Or you put on one of your standard tent dresses and it has become too small. "How depressing," you might conclude. Your husband might walk in and comment, "I'll call Army Surplus and order a new tent." He hurt your feelings, and he made you mad. Right?

Not at all, because all of your emotions are merely products of your own conscious thoughts, every single time. If external events or other people could really cause emotions, then everyone at a ball park would cheer or boo at the same time. As you know, when a player scores, only half of the audience cheers, while the others sit in restrained silence or sometimes let loose exasperated sighs or boos. If the activating event is a touchdown, the home team fans *think,* up in their brains, "Hooray! That's wonderful!" and feel and behave accordingly, while the visiting team fans think, up in their brains, "Oh, no. That's terrible," and feel and behave in a less pleasant way.

Emotions are generated by thoughts—thoughts that are highly interpretive and also highly evaluative. A home team fan may interpret and evaluate a home team touchdown as undesirable, and feel bad if, for example, the points put the home team over the point spread of his or her wager.

When, above, you hypothetically saw yourself in the mirror and found that your XXXL dress was insufficiently L and then heard the derisive remarks by your rude and insensitive husband, you were also *evaluating* yourself and *interpreting* the events according to certain beliefs. These beliefs are deeply held convictions, and you believed them fully and without reservation at the time you were emoting—that is, feeling bad, feeling hurt, and feeling angry. The bad news is that you are quite wrong—mistaken—in the deeply held convictions that led to your negative emotions.

The good news is that because you are reading this page with comprehension you obviously possess sufficient intelligence to "see through" your own irrationalities and bring about a dramatic and rapid change in your emotional life—right now. All of your emotions, no matter how pleasant or unpleasant, are caused by your own thoughts, no matter what transpires, or how disappointing or frustrating your circumstances are. Instead of having very little control over your emotions, you have enormous control over your feelings at virtually all times, fat or slim, hungry or not. In spite of your fat, you need not suffer fatness—the self-stigmatizing philosophy of worthlessness and powerlessness. Even though a loved one berates you for being fat or for being undisciplined, you are not obliged to follow suit.

7. Because I have acted poorly or harmed someone, I should moralistically blame and condemn myself,

   instead of the rational idea that as a human being I am uniquely fallible. I may feel regret, remorse, or sadness for my behavior and mistakes, but I need not conclude that I am a worthless person.

   Guilt, a gift from our parents that keeps on giving, is an emotion of childhood that would easily be outgrown if it were not powerfully reinforced throughout society. Originally, guilt is a useful, although often harmful, device for parents to control the behavior of their children when they leave the room. Later, guilt serves as a kind of "superego" or moral restraint for certain forbidden, antisocial, or illegal activities. But as one reaches adulthood the need for self-rating as a central ingredient of one's "conscience" fades, and ethical behavior may be derived from one's own human experience. Humanistic philosophy takes a far more positive view of human nature than theologically derived perceptions of the human condition.

   At the heart of the traditional Judeo-Christian view of human beings is the Doctrine of Variable Human Worth, which has it that one's intrinsic worth (worth in the universe) is a varying, quantifiable essence that is somehow to be conferred, earned, or proved. We may imagine a scale of zero to ten, representing how much worth one has at a given moment, and the indicator will slide between the numbers according to a set of rules given by certain respectable authorities. These religious rules, derived from old writings and interpreted by clergy, form what is known as "doctrine," or the conditions under which one may be grudgingly permitted to feel marginally worthwhile to himself or herself. Doctrine then becomes a wedge between *love* and *self* so that the two are never really united but only conditionally exposed to each other. The result is lifelong shame over one's personal self—an underlying feeling of badness or rottenness or inferiority that Dr. Albert Ellis wittily calls "shithood."

The elegance of Rational Recovery lies in its simple antidote to the doctrine of variable human worth. We learn, through a process of reasoning, that we can neither prove nor disprove our inherent goodness or badness, so we therefore take an elegant shortcut to self-esteem by *making it up*! That's right: We simply break certain rules because we can see that they are bogus rules. Instead of *proving* or *demonstrating* our decency, goodness, worthiness, or self-esteem, we *declare* it. Why do we simply accept ourselves, even though we are quite fallible and others may angrily condemn us? For four reasons: (1) It feels better than to hate or condemn ourselves; (2) no one can stop us from doing it; (3) it makes no sense to rate ourselves according to our performances or according to the opinions of others; and (4) it is not guilt that prevents us from behaving in antisocial or unethical ways, but our own enlightened self-interest. Guilt and shame (which are essentially the same) fade away in the light of reason. With this rational insight, self-forgiveness easily replaces self-condemnation, and the struggle for self-worth is over. Try it. You'll like it.

8. *Other people should not behave poorly, and when they do they should be blamed, moralistically condemned, and punished for their misdeeds,*

   instead of the rational idea that everyone makes mistakes and it makes no sense to blame others for their imperfections. For me to think that others are not as they should be is a failure on my part to accept reality. If I condemn or judge others, then I will apply the same measures to myself and end up with feelings of personal guilt—just like a little child.

   Most people believe that anger is an inevitable (even healthy) reaction to frustration or disappointment, especially when some other person is responsible for that frustration or disappointment. This irrationality is so common that it is built into our language— for example, "He makes me angry" or "You make me mad!" It is also common to view anger as the opposite of passivity or cowardice, which it is not, and in that way justify tantrums, rages, or aggressive and violent behavior. Cemeteries around the world are quite full of the remains of individuals who devoutly and unyieldingly believed that anger is a necessary or desirable consequence of frustration and disappointment. The remains of the victims of angry people also occupy a fair share of graves. Vital statistics for these victims as well as their assailants reflect even better than psychological theories that people act the way they feel. While anger is certainly understandable in many situations, that does not mean that anger is necessary, appropriate, helpful in any real way, or rational. Anger is neither "good" nor "bad," but people may choose to become less angry when disappointed by refusing to blame others for their poor behavior or blame fate itself. Here is a brief ABC on anger:

A: He stole my wallet.

B: He shouldn't have done that. I can't stand this kind of behavior. He should know better. He's a rotten SOB, and I'll teach him a lesson he'll never forget.

C: Anger. Verbal hostility.

D: Why shouldn't he be as he is? Why should he know better when he obviously doesn't? Is it really terrible to be stolen from? Is he really a rotten person or an SOB? How will it help me to vent anger?

E: He is not perfect. He is the way he should be, because he has never learned to act differently. He isn't worthless, although his behavior certainly is to me. I can be assertive without being verbally aggressive. I can tolerate this, although I don't much like it.

F: I am disappointed and not really angry.

Hydraulics and Generators

If you are willing to take the risk of being different from others to overcome your emotional dependence on food, then these authors suggest that you recognize the different ways to conceptualize your emotions. The "hydraulic theory" of human emotions goes something like this, given that there are many variations:

"An emotion, especially anger, is 'something down there that bothers me.' It is a pressure or force in me that makes me feel upset or behave poorly. It is caused in the present not only by frustrating events, but also by past disappointments, especially bad experiences in childhood. I have no direct control over my anger because it is just there; therefore all I can really learn to do is manage it the best I can. Anger occupies space in my guts and can build up into pressure that somehow has to get out. People can increase the pressure by doing things I don't like. If I erupt into yelling or telling people off, I can reduce the amount of anger I have. When I feel the anger coming up, I can stuff it back down, and this is repression. But the anger is still down there, building up pressure for later. When my guts are sore from too much anger, I can take away the discomfort by eating food, especially something with a strong flavor punch."

Sound familiar? Perhaps. It is quite likely that you think of your guts as a container for anger, swelling with pressure piped in from the past and from the outside world until your emotions build up and finally erupt. If so, then compare this with the *generator* theory of human emotions:

"Imagine several colored electric lights and an electric generator, with the generator representing your brain, where thinking occurs, and the colored light bulbs representing your various emotions, somewhere in your abdomen. When you have a thought, the lamps light up, in different combinations and with different intensities. The red light is anger, the blue one is depression, the green one is affection, the pink one is humor, the purple one is sexual feeling, and so on. Imagine yourself blaming someone for 'being a jerk' and thinking of how intolerable this 'jerk's' behavior is. Now imagine that the red light is glowing, representing your anger. The more you blame, the brighter and redder the red light gets. The thoughts in your brain are driving your anger. Now imagine that you find reason to forgive the character who displeased you, and see the red light dim and then go out. Now picture a sexually attractive person, and see the purple light start to glow. Now think of something funny, and notice the pink light flicker and glow. Now think something gloomy and hopeless, and see the blue light throb in cold hues. You feel the way you think. Do you see?"

This last example is the generator theory of human emotions. Simplistic? Yes, these illustrations are simplistic, but the generator concept is far more accurate in describing how the brain works than the hydraulic theory noted earlier. Not only is it more accurate, but it also provides individuals with a means finally to grasp direct control over their emotions. When it is seen that emotions, like the glowing lights, are directly activated by present thoughts, then the next logical insight is that "I may now control my emotions by thinking in a purposeful way." This purposeful way is called rational thinking and is the essence of the rational-emotive behavior therapy of Dr. Albert Ellis.

9. To feel like a worthwhile person, I must be competent, intelligent, talented, and achieving in all possible respects, and to fail in any significant way, such as by putting weight back on, is to prove what I've always suspected and feared—that I am a defective, inferior, and worthless person who can never achieve real happiness in life,

instead of the rational idea that doing is more important than doing well, trying is the first step toward succeeding, and accepting myself now as a fallible yet inestimably worthwhile human being is entirely possible.

It is nearly impossible to grow up in our nutty, irrational culture without getting at least moderately screwed up on this idea. Well-meaning parents often remark, "Someday you'll amount to something, Johnny, when you've gotten yourself established and have a family of your own." Johnny can hardly avoid the implication that, for now, his worth is being rated at zero by his parent, and he may approach life's involvements with the irrational agenda of trying to get rid of the idea that he is worthless. Life, in this perspective, is largely a proving ground to sort out the worthy from the worthless, and this struggle to prove somehow that one is worthwhile continues very often until one's death. An education may be undertaken more to enhance self-esteem than for the more rational purposes of learning itself and vocational preparation. Sexual relationships may be undertaken more to prove manliness and prowess than for the more rational purpose of obtaining sexual pleasure and cultivating intimacy. A career may represent a challenge to demonstrate power, competence, and control, and one's earnings may become a symbol of one's intrinsic worth rather than one's financial worth. Retirement or disability may pose a compounded threat for people whose self-esteem is entangled with productivity and ambition.

Once again, REBT asserts that one's essential worth is self-determined and that one need not be successful, talented, or achieving to consider oneself worthwhile. A common objection to this concept is that if one isn't "driven" to succeed by the desire to feel successful, then motivation to succeed will be squelched. The pleasant irony here is that quite the opposite is so. If your sense of well-being is on the line when you undertake challenging tasks, then you may be reluctant to risk the pain that would seem to be caused by failure. You may feel insecure and lack "self-confidence" when approaching difficult tasks or projects. After all, a lot seems at stake: your self-esteem. However, if you can see that failing cannot make you into a failure, but only a fallible person whom you will continue to respect, then it will become much easier to take the risk of tackling a difficult problem. In Rational Recovery, your self-confidence is based on your ability to fail rather than succeed! Even in your social affairs, you may apply this way of thinking so that rejection has no bearing on your opinion of yourself. And in your sexual life, you may find that your performance in the hay is enhanced when you relax about the prospect of failure, rather than worry about how awful it would be if part of your body did not function just perfectly at just the right time.

Naturally, your efforts to establish and maintain a steady, desirable weight will be much easier when you get your ego off the hook. Another Achilles' heel of overeaters seeking weight control is the "surrender response" that seems to take hold after a limited indulgence in forbidden food. Some theorists call this phenomenon the "abstinence violation effect," wherein one senses, "I'm over the line! I've really gone and done it, now, so I may as well go whole hog. . . ." The underlying theme in most relapses is the irrational idea that the failure by bingeing somehow proves what you have always suspected, that you are a loser, a weak-willed washout who can never achieve a sense of genuine self-respect.

Some counselors and therapists perpetuate this kind of nonsense in their offices when they suggest that people who suffer feelings of inadequacy draw up a list of things that are "good" about themselves, such as "I am honest, kind, cheerful, have a good sense of humor, never hurt animals, and like to help people." The subtle, irrational idea here is that positive attributes and competencies are required for self-acceptance, and if one can just make a sufficiently long list of "good" things, it will outweigh the apparent evidence for one's sense of personal inferiority. This is what is sometimes called "neurotic agreement" between therapist and client, and whatever relief from distress the client may get, it will likely be of very short duration. You may have attempted to lose weight as an avenue to self-acceptance, only to find that you can feel miserable about yourself no matter which belt notch is currently in use. Thus, when a binge "happens," it is quite easy to conclude that you are a failure and that your quest for self-esteem is hopeless. Then your surrender to your appetite for comforting food—the Feast Beast—is complete.

The rational conclusion, after you discover that there is no way to "prove" your intrinsic worth, is forthrightly to *accept* yourself, imperfections, fallibilities, and all, in the present moment, thus taking an instant shortcut to the cherished feelings of self-acceptance. This requires that you not be unduly concerned about the approval of others and be willing to violate social norms, for this rational insight is a rarity in present times.

10. If "things" aren't the way I want them very much to be, then it's terrible, horrible, awful, and catastrophic,

instead of the rational idea that "terrible" and "awful" are magical words meaning "worse than most unfortunate." Since nothing can be more than 100 percent bad, "things" don't have to be any particular way for me to remain relatively calm. If I cannot change or control conditions, I can accept any misfortune, including, when finally necessary, death.

Understanding that nothing truly terrible can possibly happen is a rational insight that can have a greater calming effect than belief in a *rescuing* deity. Understanding reality is manifestly more useful than being inappropriately dependent on an ethereal being.

Let's use an example to illustrate how the ABC's work in Rational Recovery. In your RR-Fatness groups, you will be encouraged to learn this unique process for bringing about desired change in yourself. You may use a blank sheet of paper to do the ABC's, but RRS provides Rational Spreadsheets to aid in applying the ABC's. Another explanation of the ABC's is presented in Chapter 4, "Eating Correctly."

When threatening circumstances develop, ask yourself, "What's the worst thing that can happen?" and then know that your worst fears are unfounded; you are built to accept, tolerate, or endure great hardship without dying, going insane, or suffering injury or loss that would preclude any further good in life. For example, you may fret and worry endlessly about the possibility of **A,** going bankrupt. "Look at these bills!" you say, telling yourself at point **B,** *"Isn't it awful* that I don't have enough money to pay them off this month! How will I ever take care of this? If I don't get control of my finances, I'll go bankrupt, *and that would be horrible!"* The consequence is considerable anxiety and an inclination to binge on food; the financial problem is in no way helped. Your rational alternative is to **D**(ispute) the **B**(aloney) by asking yourself, "Supposing I can't pay all of this month's bills? Is that my problem, or my creditors'? And if I get dunned, or lose my credit rating, would that really be *terrible*? Or would it just be a pain in the ass for a few years and prevent me from accumulating more debts? And suppose I go bankrupt. Would I die? Would I even have to suffer? If I had to live in a small apartment instead of this nice, big house, would I have to be miserable? Hell, no. I can have some great times no matter where I live and no matter how much money I have. I would be more restricted and have more inconveniences and fewer luxuries, but I doubt that my family or I would starve. Millions of people go bankrupt, and life goes on reasonably well for many of them. Even if I had to go on welfare, I could still get lots of good out of life, even though that would not be ideal. But the chances of bankruptcy are small anyway. If I pay a little to each account each month, maybe I can prevent it. But if the worst happens anyway, I honestly believe that I can handle it!" In this rich vein of rational thinking, one turns one's life over to *oneself* instead of to some external authority, to a Higher Power, or to the whims of fortune.

By **D**isputing the irrational ideas behind your disturbed emotions, as above, you will "see through" your problems and experience the **E**ffect of feeling relieved and being able to think about creative solutions to your money problems. You will no longer be able to "awfulize" what is really just an unfortunate, perplexing problem. This rational approach can be applied to virtually any problem, and the general effect is drastically to lower your anxiety level as well as any inclination you may have to overeat. Always remember your ABC's. And don't forget D and E!

When you believe something is terrible or awful, you are engaged in magical thinking. You may be interested to know that the word "terrible" has no meaning in any dictionary. Look it up yourself. It is what dictionary makers call a *tautology,* or a word that is defined by another word that has the same meaning. The definitions of "terrible" include "awful," "dreadful," "fearsome," and "horrible," but when you look up those words, they list "terrible" plus the others. Then each definition takes the root of the magical word and says, "That which inspires _____ (terror, horror, dread, fear)." But we are learning that *nothing* at point A causes *anything* at point C and that it is only what we *believe* at point B that can make anything seem "terrible."

For many, it is difficult to grasp that nothing terrible happens in life and only one's thinking makes it seem so, and they view the rational viewpoint as a denial of reality and a position of cold, stupid detachment. "Terrible things *do* happen," they say. "What about the Vietnam War, or the Armenian earthquake? Suppose your house burns down? What about when a loved one dies, or you're sued for everything you have? Suppose you're sent to prison? Aren't *those* things terrible?"

To answer this with a question, "For whom, and how much, and for how long?" Let's use the example of an earthquake disaster. The victims in a natural disaster all react differently; some are immobilized with *panic* or *despondency,* and others who are relatively unfazed by the urgent situation function as leaders and heroes. In a natural disaster the victims are *startled* and there is much *excitement* and *alarm.* Those who are *mourning* the *loss* of their homes and *loved* ones feel great *sadness* and *helplessness,* and this may be followed later by *depression.* The injured feel *pain* and they *fear* for life and limb. Their lives may never be the same, and they may *grieve* for their losses for many years. Do we really add to our understanding of human tragedy by saying "It's terrible"? We can compassionately recognize the emotions of those who are suffering without calling a natural disaster "terrible" or "awful." (Besides, natural disasters create work for people, who are often paid handsomely for their efforts. It is hardly terrible for them. Children are sometimes seen playing happily in the ruins of earthquakes. Many of these children seem little perturbed at the devastation of their community. They somehow have missed that "It's terrible.") Would a Martian or lunar earthquake be terrible? Of course not; "terrible" is a human perception, one that always overgeneralizes and always exceeds reality.

To achieve dietary discipline for weight loss and weight maintenance it is important to maintain a steady emotional footing. Life is full of frustration, hardships, losses, and disappointments, and there is usually some misfortune in the works that can be magnified into a catastrophe that could justify relapse into bingeing.

Certainly we feel strong emotions over loss, and grieving is the "deawfulization" of what we originally perceived as terrible. When grief is complete, one has concluded that the loss is no longer terrible. The intensity and the duration of grief can be strongly influenced by reason. In fact, grief, often thought of as a pouring out of sadness until none is left, can better be seen as a process of reality testing wherein one changes one's belief from "I can't live happily without so-and-so" to "I may always miss so-and-so, but I guess I can still enjoy my life." Consequently, the ability to reason aggressively (think rationally) can decrease both the intensity and the duration of personal grief.

11. It is easier to avoid than to face squarely certain self-responsibilities, such as reducing the amount of food I ingest and concentrating on personal growth,

instead of the rational idea that the "easy way," especially continuing to overeat, is invariably much harder and more painful in the long run.

- "I'm not quite ready yet."
- "I have to work through some personal things before I diet. Otherwise I'll just be wasting my time and all the effort."
- "I just got these new XXL dresses and I want to wear them for a while."
- "There's just too much going on in my life right now. I couldn't stick to anything I started right now."

These Feast Beast utterances assure you of a continuous supply of the concentrated food that you now plan to eat with impunity for as long as your frame will support your weight.

Overeaters struggle with this self-defeating idea because the compulsion is perpetuated by the desire for immediate gratification. Enough has been said on that. But RR is more than a slim-down program; it's also a program for *staying* at your chosen weight.

Happiness is rarely achieved through inaction and inertia. As you recover from fatness you will find that food played a very central role in your life and that it is difficult to find new ways to have fun. You will continue for some time to think that having a binge would be wonderful and that it is important to feel satiated to enjoy yourself. If you are unable to have fun, you are likely to have a relapse binge.

Consequently, it is critical that you overcome what stands between you and fun. Most of us find pleasure in other people, in special relationships, and in social and recreational activities. Others find great enjoyment in creative pursuits, in aesthetic pleasures, in sexual activities, in special projects such as organizations and politics, or in physical fitness projects. There is so much more to life than food, once one overcomes the philosophy of fatness.

Let's face it: Making new friends is hard. But it is far easier to take the risks of meeting new people, people who are not necessarily food people, by eliminating the perceived risk of rejection. All through *Taming the Feast Beast* and in ideas 5 and 7, as described on pages 97–99 and 101–102, you will find something that is unique and delightful about Rational Recovery. You will find that by just loving yourself as the real, living thing you are, for no particular reason other than that it feels better than *not* loving yourself, you will be much more at ease around others, you will honestly not care greatly whether they like you or approve of you. By not *needing* the approval of others you will be able to *be yourself*, to say what you think, and to express yourself without shyness, apprehension, or fear of rejection. The pleasant irony here is that the more you are just yourself, dropping all pretensions and just being what you are, the more people will tend to like you, accept you, and value your company. Conversely, the more you think you *need* friends, approval, companionship, and affection, the more you'll put people off and the *fewer* friends you'll have.

As you recover from fatness, you have an obligation to yourself to pursue your own self-defined goals. Because you're already certain of your individual worth, you won't be tackling projects to prove that you're as good as other people. If, for example, you were to return to school, it wouldn't be to erase feelings of inferiority about your fatness or your lack of academic achievement but rather to open the door of opportunity to goals that you, in your own opinion, want and deserve. Your sexual strivings will be for your own personal gratification rather than to prove your masculinity or femininity or to prove to yourself and others that you're lovable rather than sexually defective. Your very life, then, becomes an opportunity for self-fulfillment, a time for getting the good things in life for yourself, enjoying others, and for meaningful activities and pursuits. Life is *better* than a bowl of cherries! Go for it! This life's for you!

12. Because I am down a few pounds, I absolutely must not gain them back, no matter what, because then I will be defeated and the struggle will become hopeless,

   instead of the rational idea that as time in Rational Recovery goes by, overeating comes to appear increasingly stupid because of the obvious selfish advantages of prudent eating. When I do occasionally overeat, however, it won't be awful or terrible because I will then resume correct eating—selfishly, guiltlessly, and very quickly.

   This irrational idea, that having one binge with weight gain means failure and will lead to additional weight gain, may serve to deter some of us from overeating, but for others it is probably just a self-fulfilling prophecy. The idea, incidentally, is irrational because it fails the test of objective truth. Many overeaters impulsively eat too much, then stop without resuming the binge pattern. Those people understand that perfectionism is the enemy of weight control, and occasional incorrect eating is not only harmless, but even desirable for long-term success. They understand that the "chipping" phenomenon, where one seems to tempt fate with a doughnut or banana split, need not lead to gluttony and catastrophic weight gain. But alas, chippers too often hear the newly energized voice of the Feast Beast saying, "There! Now you've really gone and done it! There's no use stopping now. You are out of control! It's time really to pig out, so you might as well enjoy it."

   Some of you may have heard of the Elizabeth Taylor Diet, which includes a scheduled once-weekly binge. Here Liz seems to be recognizing the problem of sustaining discipline over time, and she asserts the dieter's freedom to "fall off the wagon" from time to time. To *schedule* self-defeating acts, however, is questionable; it would seem better from a rational viewpoint simply to accept occasional lapses in correct eating, if and when they occur—and with the constant self-assurance that each "forbidden bite" is fully under one's control. One exercise in *rational* self-control could be to, just once in a long while, very planfully have "just one" of something—a piece of candy, a bite of cake, or one potato chip. Until the aftertaste fades away, your Feast Beast voice may beg and plead for more, but this time you will be well equipped to recognize it and repel its advances. Despite ads to the contrary, human beings are quite capable of having just one of something that is tasty or salty.

In RR you are encouraged to reject ideas of ever achieving perfection, even though you may eat correctly for long periods. Because of the difficulty of sustained discipline, you will, probably, from time to time, eat excessively or consume incorrect foods. At these times you can help yourself by avoiding the "abstinence violation effect," in which overeaters catastrophize over eating errors and plunge headlong into self-destructive eating with powerlessness on their minds.

13. Because I am substantially overweight from overeating, I need something or someone other than or greater than myself on which to rely,
instead of the rational idea that dependency is my original problem, and it is better to start now to take the risks of thinking and acting independently.

All through *Taming the Feast Beast,* you will find references to *dependence* as a chief culprit in overeating and overweight. As you reread *Taming the Feast Beast,* you will become more aware of how various dependencies sabotage your own best interests. Following are several dependency angles you may have overlooked thus far.

Why do you want to lose weight in the first place? Is it to please others, or yourself? Is it because someone thinks you should? Are you trying to impress someone else, or yourself? Do you have a "right" to overeat and to be overweight? I hope you understand that you have the "right" to do most anything you please in life— as long as you are willing to accept the consequences.

Do you involve others in your struggle to eat correctly? Your chances of learning to eat correctly are far less when you depend on someone else to keep your balance. The next time you think of saying to your spouse, "Let's go on a diet together," or "How do you expect me to lose weight with the freezer full of your ice cream?" imagine yourself and your spouse walking a tightwire, tugging and pulling at each other to keep each other from falling. It might be nice if "true love" could serve the personal interests of both partners in a marital relationship, but that's the stuff of romance novels—fiction, and certainly not real life. If yours is a loving relationship, then it would be more appropriate to express your devotion by not dragging your loved one into an issue as personal as what you put in your mouth.

Another dependency that may needlessly complicate your efforts to check your intake of food is dependence on a rescuing deity. In Rational Recovery, *belief* in some Higher Power or Supreme Being is a different matter from *dependence* on such an entity. In Rational Recovery, we leave whatever gods there are to their other godly duties, such as creating universes, tending to the courses of rivers, and seeing to it that each flower is the proper color. To depend on a god or Higher Power to stop us from eating too much is not only setting that deity up for failure but also fostering dependence in an area of our own competence. This is neither character-building nor useful.

Even strongly religious people find RR to be an ideal solution to weight control, because rationality is congruent with their theological beliefs. For example, one man from an RR-Fatness group commented, "I am a Christian. I believe that Jesus Christ is my personal Savior, and when I have a flat tire, I immediately get down on my knees. But, you see, I don't get on my knees to pray. It's to turn the lug wrench. When I pray, it's to worship, and not to ask for help with things that are *mine* to do—no matter how difficult. I like RR, because it keeps me honest with myself in areas in which I'm tempted to become dependent."

For a great many people, god images seem to intrude into everyday problems in ways that are unhelpful. For example, many overweight people think that they are being "tested" or "punished" by a cosmic being, or that eventual thinness will result from submitting to such a being. This kind of belief system usually gets started in childhood and remains resistant to change throughout life, but many people overcome *childlike* religious beliefs as a matter of self-improvement. One very popular weight reduction program that encourages its participants to seek supernatural aid in daily living is Overeaters Anonymous. Their famous twelve steps start with a confession of powerlessness over their impulses to overeat, and then the program unfolds as a deepening dependency on some Higher Power. People who don't accept supernatural ideas are encouraged to accept the group as a Higher Power, which, from a rational viewpoint, would seem a most unwise choice. On many crucial points Overeaters Anonymous says just the opposite from Rational Recovery, so people of different opinions now have a clear choice on the road to recovery. A person of any religion or no religion may find RR quite helpful. Your religion/spirituality is your own business and is certainly not a requirement for controlling the ingestion of food or other substances.

14. Because fatness once greatly affected my life, it will continue to affect me frequently and indefinitely,
    instead of the rational idea that self-acceptance is self-fulfilling. Because there is so much more to life than a constant struggle to lose weight, I can gradually close the book on that sorry chapter in my life and become vitally absorbed in activities and projects outside of myself that are unrelated to my biological appetites and physical dimensions.
    Research shows that many of us are "naturally fat" while others have no tendency to convert calories to excess pounds. Even so, correct eating will *by definition* result in a comfortable body of "normal" proportions. In Rational Recovery we make friends with our bodies and come to terms with our appetites for food in such a way that learning is self-reinforcing and durable. By "seeing through" the irrational philosophy of fatness that has sustained our overweight condition, we are most unlikely to revert to something that no longer makes sense. Once the freedom of emotional independence is experienced, the slavery of dependence is history.
    This is not to say that there will not be variations of weight, or that one will *never* binge on food, or feel hurt or angry or depressed. That vision would suggest that one had achieved a perfect solution to life's problems, a kind of mortal sainthood to which

only the heavenbound would aspire. Rational Recovery simply provides a set of skills for correcting problems when they occur and, when possible or convenient, preventing them in the first place. Once learned, these skills remain intact over a lifetime, like swimming or riding a bike.

15. The reasons for my overweight condition are buried in my past and in my immensely fascinating and complex psyche. I am overeating for reasons that only very intelligent and highly educated persons can understand,
 instead of the rational idea that calories are transformed into fat, and my overweight is directly related to the kinds of food I eat and the number of surplus calories I ingest per unit of time. While I may have learned some patterns of self-defeat in the past, my present overweight and emotional disturbances are caused entirely by my present personal philosophy.

Chapter 2 is a discussion of the mythology that surrounds eating disorders, especially the common idea that one's past is an all-important determinant of present problems. Suffice it to say that the past does not exist except symbolically today in memories, in learned ideas, and in behaviors. Much attention is given to the origins of people's problems, when the solutions lie in the present. Rational Recovery provides a means to instigate change now, and each person is given the *information* that is relevant to desired change.

Getting better from fatness involves aggressive reasoning, and usually people sense that they are going into uncharted waters. Indeed, recovery often requires that one give up certain ideas that seem more important than food itself! Years of struggling with an eating disorder contribute to a self-concept based on many failures and many explanations from experts everywhere, including talk shows, magazines, newspapers, psychologists, medical doctors, and celebrities. All of these add up to a *gestalt,* or a "big picture" of the nature of the problem of overeating. All is explained, yet nothing really helps.

The chief difficulty is that no one, including the overeater, seems to hold the overeater *accountable* for what is placed in the mouth. The guilt-ridden overeater is not holding himself or herself accountable, but is indulging in victimhood after the fact of overeating. Rational Recovery, which may be likened to a crash course in growing up, turns the participant's energies directly onto the immediate problem of eating correctly. There is pleasure in the idea that one is a *victim* of the past, of bad genes, of poor metabolism, of childhood trauma, of riotous appetites, or of exotic mental traits that distinguish one from others. Giving up the idea that one's uniqueness is the cause of chronic overeating, in favor of the idea that one's thinking is immature, irrational, sloppy, or downright false, is the central challenge in Rational Recovery. Understanding "why" does not, in itself, bring about change.

Fatness, for better or worse, is *identity,* and to challenge one's self-concept is difficult and sometimes fearsome. The saying "Inside every fat person is a slim one trying to get out" isn't far off the mark, but the key insight in Rational Recovery is that neither the fat self nor the slim self is the *you* that is within the skin. Regardless of your past, your physical dimensions, or your personality makeup, you may now reinvent yourself as a fallible yet inestimably worthwhile person. No expert can do this for you; all it takes is you.

16. Somewhere out there is a perfect antidote to life's problems, and until I find it, I am doomed to a life of uncertainty and turmoil,
instead of the rational idea that uncertainty is the spice of life, and seeking a perfect solution is silly and a waste of time. I will do better to view life as an enjoyable experiment, seeking my own pleasures and my own personal growth.

It certainly would be nice if there were good answers to grand questions such as "What's the meaning of life?" Unfortunately, we seem no nearer to answering broad philosophical questions about ultimate reality than in the past, even though many softheaded gurus and ecclesiastical authorities make continuous claims of perfect knowledge. Rational Recovery makes no claim of perfect truth and offers no elevated state of being as a reward for thinking rationally. We seek salvation from nothing but our own irrationality, and we do not strive for a sense of well-being that exceeds that of being reasonably happy most of the time. Few of us expect to benefit from being dead, but prefer to live this life to the fullest. We generally accept our own ignorance on many questions and prefer a sense of wonderment to trying to fill the blank spaces in our understanding with spiritual ideas, as required by OA. We know that just being human is quite sufficient to justify feelings of worth—regardless of our failings, shortcomings, and imperfections.

Rational Recovery is not a perfect solution to life's problems, nor is it an endless quest for salvation from the human condition, for serenity, nirvana, or oneness with all. Instead, it is a time-limited program for coming to terms with some central life issues so that one may leave the group with improved self-understanding and some new strategies for getting more out of life. People who begin on their journey toward rationality usually find new horizons before them, so that as time passes personal growth continues in pleasantly unexpected ways. RR vindicates people who have been convinced that they are worthless, powerless, or less fit to live life on their own terms, and RR also emancipates people from self-limiting concepts of self. There are limitations to self-help that are well documented in professional literature, so you may do well to seek professional counseling or therapy if it seems that reading this book and participation in Rational Recovery meetings fall short of the mark.

I don't want her
You can have her
She's too fat for me.
She's too fat.
She's too fat.
She's too fat for me.
—Arthur Godfrey

CHAPTER 7

Sex and Fat

Goodness. Here are two of the most emotionally charged words in the English language, together in the same chapter title. What could the authors be up to here? Are they going to suggest that sex and fat don't mix? Or are they going to suggest that there is no contradiction between being fat and having good sex? Read on and see.

First, let's be honest. Most people want to look good to the opposite sex, whether they are single or married. It's just human nature. In the order of things, sexual attraction is the mechanism for the survival of the human species, and those who are more attractive to the opposite sex are more likely to produce offspring than those who are less attractive or distinctly unattractive. Like it or not, obese people are at a real disadvantage in attracting potential sexual partners. This is also true for obese gays and lesbians.

But there's much more to sexuality than breeding. Sex is pleasure, and no sex is usually disappointing and frustrating. Sex is an important ingredient in marriage relationships, and married or not, every day is a sexual experience. We *are* our genders, regardless of more politically correct opinions, regardless of sexual orientation, and notwithstanding the exotic claims of transsexuals. Gender is a state of being that is the opposite of the other gender. For example, it is simply impossible for a man or woman, in spite of great understanding and sensitivity, to know what it is like to *be* of the opposite gender. This, we believe, is stating the obvious. And in a very real way, our bodies are an expression of our gender, our selves, and our sexuality.

Let me digress to give some examples and background.

In 1992, I (L.T.) attended the gay-lesbian parade in San Francisco. This is an annual festival that receives little media attention because of its counterculture displays of sexuality in public. The parade is probably best known because of the annual appearance of "Dykes on Bikes," roaring slowly, four abreast, down Market Street—naked. Well, almost naked. Bare-breasted, for sure. But this year one of the most popular floats was "Fat Dykes." Several four-hundred-pound lesbians stood or reclined in seductive poses, scantily clad, letting it be known that they were intensely sexual as well as very fat. Beauty is in the eye of the beholder, and I saw physical beauty as well as beauty of the human condition among the heavies who glided down Market Street that day. They were pretty, and they seemed to *feel* pretty. I doubt that all of them were equally comfortable in the cool, foggy air with throngs of onlookers, but they were there, making their statements for the benefit of others of their kind, and having fun at it.

As the parade of bare-breasted, bountiful beauties passed by, I thought, "These women are gutsy in more ways than one. Not only are they struggling against the stigma of being lesbians in a homophobic society, but also against the stigma of fatness."

Then I flashed—mentally, of course—on a TV program I had seen only days before. It was a tabloid talk show featuring five obese women who complained bitterly about how their obesity was ruining their relationships with men. Each had her spouse or lover seated beside her, and they, too, lamented the loss of intimacy on account of adipose tissue. One woman, Helen, had become celibate from shame alone, and told of wretched feelings she experiences each time she sees herself in the mirror. She shamefully darkens the bathroom to bathe, and has removed mirrors elsewhere that would reflect her image. Her husband says he loves her and cares deeply for her, but has released her from any sexual obligation, and now resorts to masturbation for sexual release. He says he is attracted to her and would have no complaint about her obese condition if she would consent to sex. But he accepts her hypermodesty and that theirs is a lost sexual love. Helen, explaining that she is out of control, wistfully accepts that she will probably eat herself to death and explains that the end is probably near —the end of her, and thus of the relationship.

Another of the five, much less overweight than Helen, was angry at herself and her husband, and she told of the hopelessness of her life-threatening condition. Kate felt worthless and resented her husband's critical attitude. He described how he wants her to lose weight and become more like the girl he married, and he makes frequent offers to go on a diet with her. He dutifully proposes that "with her permission" he supervise her eating by serving her portions and watching over her during meals. To discourage overeating, he would verbally reprimand her, and if that didn't work, he would politely remove the remaining food from the table. He also generously offered to do the shopping and cooking so she wouldn't have to expose herself to what he called "the addictive substance." He told the audience how good-looking she was until she married him, and wondered aloud if she wasn't overeating just to cause him trouble. Sex? "Not on your life," he said, and he launched off on a lecture on how erections are not under the control of their owners and how a certain amount of attractiveness is necessary for coitus to transpire. He said he loves her so much he wants her to lose weight for her own good. She revealed to the millions who watched that he also called her names and was never affectionate. She admitted that at times she felt like murdering him, but at those times she would have a free-falling sense of worthlessness, along with renewed craving for high-calorie foods.

Helen and Kate both are fat, celibate, miserable, and hopeless. Helen's husband is willing and able to have sex, but she isn't. She is too ashamed of her body for physical intimacy, and she cannot believe that he would obtain any pleasure from sexual activity with her. She cannot tolerate being seen, by herself or by her husband, and sexual intimacy is too threatening even to contemplate. She is rejected by herself and by her masturbating husband, and she imagines herself eating herself into oblivion—alone.

Kate, however, is willing to have sex, but her husband isn't. He is ashamed of her body, and he disturbs himself with the idea that her fatness is causing him to be impotent. He rejects her, rather sadistically to symbolize who is responsible for his impotency, and she then binges to cope with feelings of rejection, all the while becoming fatter and fatter.

So, standing in the fog of San Francisco, I wondered, "What is the difference, in very simple terms, between those tortured souls on TV and the cheerful lovey-lumps on the Fat Dykes float?" Were the big, bulky broads blessed with more intelligence? Had the challenge of being different brought out the best in them? Did they come from more functional families that filled them with love? Had they found that only another fat woman could love a fat woman? The liberated lesbians, while their sexual life-style may not inspire the majority, may hold a key for men and women who are unhappy in their big, bulky bodies.

The rather extreme examples above are only a matter of degree. There is a myth that fat and sex don't mix. People who believe this not only get less sexual satisfaction (or none!) but also suffer from the self-perpetuating condition we call fatness.

Love More and Eat Less for Delicious Sex

Believe it or not, sex is the primary motivator for most of the millions who fret endlessly about their diets. They want to look sexy so they can have sexual relations and feel like a desirable sex partner. There is nothing wrong with either appetite, for food or for sex, and ideally each reader will satisfy both of them. But ironically, the same people who want to become sexually attractive also say that they overeat because they aren't or weren't loved enough. "I eat when I'm lonesome" is a common remark among fatties, as well as "Food is my friend. It's always there when I feel lonesome." Sexually rejected fatsos complain, "Why can't he/she love me for who I am, rather than for my body?" But, again ironically, they are also the ones who reject *themselves* because of too many pounds in the wrong places.

One need not be slim and shapely to enjoy the finest sexual pleasures. Indeed, only your imagination limits your sexual activity when you are overweight. If you imagine that your fat rolls are disgusting to your partner, and if you dwell on fat modesty during intimate encounters, then you will have less fun. And if you avoid intimate encounters to avoid fat-modesty embarrassment, then you will have little sexual fun.

Do It

Male or female, whether or not you ever lose weight, you may choose to be more sexually adventurous. In your own privacy, you may get in touch with your body along the lines described in *The Joy of Sex* by Alex Comfort. Apply the attitudes in that book to yourself. Caress your body, touch the fat areas on your abdomen, thighs, and arms, feel how you feel being felt. Find at least one erogenous zone that is fat. It may be on your stomach, thighs, shoulders, neck, or anywhere. In other words, find a fat area that feels good being touched. Imagine someone else doing the touching. Make yourself learn that it's okay to be fat and feel sexy, that there is no contradiction in this. If possible, find a sexual partner with whom to take sexual risks, and get yourself to enjoy the pleasure in comfort. When you find yourself wondering what your spouse or sex partner is thinking, get back to basics and ask yourself if you are in bed to please yourself or your partner. Remember that much pleasure for your partner is in watching your own arousal. Cut loose and enjoy.

The great advantage to doing this now, before you lose an ounce, is that if you wait until you are somewhat slimmer you may still feel uptight. You may feel, as millions of American men and women feel, that you are never slim and trim enough to relax in the sexual company of another.

Eating to Orgasm

As you shed pounds, you will benefit by finding new pleasures, such as dancing, sports, sex, or just walking and looking good.

There is a trade-off in Rational Recovery, where one special pleasure is sacrificed for others. For a broader enjoyment of life, including having more sexual orgasms, eating to orgasm must go.

Never heard of eating to orgasm? Really? Of course you know what this means. You do it every time you sit before a plate. True, it isn't a sexual orgasm, with that specific sensation of genital or sexual pleasure. The eating orgasm is the "buzz" you get when you are chowing down. The phenomenon is not unlike sexual orgasms in several ways. There is a period of restlessness, then a state of arousal, often followed by some foreplay (food preparation, tasting, appetizers), then the main course, then the point of no return (the eating orgasm), and finally the satiation and relaxed, peaceful state.

The Eating Orgasm Itself

You can prevent eating orgasms by being self-conscious while you eat. You may notice, as you consume what is on your plate, that you are becoming progressively more absorbed in eating; that you are savoring the food in a rather inappropriate—excessive—way; that you are *staring* at the food as you eat—perhaps even hunched over it; that you are preparing the next bite as you chew the last; that you *absolutely love* what you are eating; that you are eating faster and faster; that you aren't really listening to or understanding the conversation around you; that you want more and more of the food you are eating; that it could use just a little salt because your taste buds are getting numbed; and that you wish you could keep eating this food forever because it is so wonderful and tasty and goooood. And then your plate is empty and you haven't had quite enough and your eyes dart for the serving dish, and you size up the portions left, and you think that you *must* have just a little more of this wonderful dish, and you take a little then just a little more to get that heavenly, heavy feeling—"I think I've had enough." But then, when the afterglow subsides, one may hear in thought, "Was this worth it? I want to be somewhere else. I really shouldn't have done this."

Rational Recovery from fatness is quite like coitus interruptus as a way of preventing the *appearance* of being pregnant. It is entirely harmless, but is only a *little* frustrating once you get the hang of it. Here are some tips to avoid "coming" at the dinner table:

1. Imagine an "enjoyment meter," appearing like a speedometer. Clock yourself so that you never go over the 55-miles-per-hour speed limit. The example above showed an eater going about 110 miles per hour. Slow down.

2. Keep up your end of the conversation unless it is about how absolutely wonderful the food is. Talk in complete sentences, and never talk with your mouth full.

3. Put your utensil down between bites. Look up. Smile at others. If alone, just smile.

4. On the table facing you, put a tiny sign that says, "It's only food." If you won't risk the opinions of others on this, then repeat to yourself while you are eating, "I promise I won't come. It's only food."

5. If you start on a binge orgasm, as described above, do the cold water treatment on yourself. *Get up from the table. "Eatus" interruptus!* Do anything. Go to the rest room and think it over. Fill a salt shaker. Take some dirty dishes to the kitchen. ET, call home.

6. Start with what looks like a disappointingly small portion, but one that will obviously keep you alive until the next meal. Imagine from the start that you will leave one bite on the plate when you are finished eating. Then do it! Even if it's filet mignon, leave a bite on your plate and push it away. Imagine—a sautéed scampi left on the plate. Down the garbage disposal. Is this cruel? You bet it is.

But we believe that people are *competent* to accept the challenges of self-reliance and self-control. Dietary discipline is akin to understanding that one would not engage in sex in inappropriate places, with the wrong people, at the wrong time. We play by rules with which we agree. We know that one may make a plan, a Big Plan, *never* to have an eating orgasm at the dinner table again, and then stick to that decision year after year, with little real discomfort, little if any whining, and with increasing appreciation of the *virtue* of moderation in food intake.

Mind Your Manners

A little-known connection between etiquette and weight control is that the rules of polite restraint recommended by well-known authorities on etiquette such as Emily Post or Miss Manners are incompatible with bingeing. Read a book on etiquette, and you will notice a distinctive air of aloofness from food itself that comes from paying attention to the context of a meal rather than the content. Indeed, etiquette serves the purpose of inhibiting "beastly" behavior by setting down rules that are enforced by social sanctions and disapproval. If your posture at the table is mannerly, you will not lean over your plate, propping yourself up with your elbows. You will engage in conversation, never speaking with food in your mouth. This automatically slows down your intake, allowing for a better appreciation of the food as well as the use of less food to ease hunger. Naturally, the Feast Beast will be able to pursue its agenda even under the controlled conditions of formal dining, but by minding your manners you may find yet another means of taming the Feast Beast.

CHAPTER 8

A Thin Chapter for the Thin Ones

You, as an anorexic, also suffer from fatness. Strange but true. Just as with those who eat too much, it is your obsession with your body image and your dependency on the opinions of others that is at the root of your trouble with eating correctly. As you read through this book, most, but not all, of the material will apply to you, and you can overcome your eating disorder by applying the general principles herein.

However, you will *not* have the difficulty overweight people may have in becoming friendly with the sensation of hunger. You have already accomplished that, even to the extent that you endanger your health—even your life. For you, hunger is like a drug, and when you feel hungry, if and when you do at all, you feel *too* good. Therefore, simply ignore those sections that encourage you to cultivate hunger and eat less, and eat correctly. That means eating *at least* three meals a day, with nourishing food at each meal, at the right times and at the right places. Plan sensible meals, and when you find yourself having eating symptoms, listen to the Beast of Belittlement.

Your Beast will sound different from that of a fat person's. It will tell you how worthless you are and suggest that you deserve more punishment than you can provide for yourself. You will feel fat and ashamed of yourself even though you are quite underweight. Your Feast Beast is spurred on by your appetite for self-punishment and it is driven by your philosophy of guilt and shame, as exemplified in the Doctrine of Variable Human Worth. According to this doctrine, your worth as a human being is something that varies according to certain conditions. As conditions fluctuate, so does your sense of personal worth—your self-esteem. Like the overeater, you also are obsessed with your physical self, and you dwell on such things as appearance and body size.

When you refuse to eat, you sometimes believe you are "being good" and that you will feel better about yourself by losing a little more weight. At other times you believe that by starving yourself you are "being bad," or at least punishing yourself for being bad. When you malnourish yourself, your body draws desperately on energy reserves until you are in an altered state of consciousness that is caused by the release of hormones and other brain chemicals. You then feel "high" and mistakenly conclude that your self-starving path to self-esteem works. At these times you are acutely ill and urgently need medical care.

For you, it would be better to weight the irrational ideas in order of importance so that you can get a sense of priority as you read *Taming the Feast Beast.* Here are suggestions on some ideas to concentrate on, starting with the idea that is probably most important:

1. The reasons for my anorexia, purging, and/or underweight condition are buried in my past and in my immensely fascinating and complex psyche. These self-destructive behaviors have causes that only very intelligent and highly educated persons can understand,
instead of the rational idea that I am eating poorly as a way of showing how little I now care for myself. I may have learned to despise myself during my childhood, but the past no longer exists. Therefore I can now think independently about myself as an adult. My obsession with being thin comes partly from the silly idea that it would be terrible if others, especially of the opposite sex, rejected me, and also from the equally silly idea that it is shameful to be overweight. By overcoming these dependencies and adding some discipline to my thinking, I can overcome my eating disorder.

2. I have little control over my feelings and emotions, which are some-how forced on me by others or external events,

instead of the rational idea that I feel the way I think and so have enormous control over my emotions, my sorrows, and my disturbances. (See idea 6, Chapter 6.)

Your problem is compounded by the fact that you do have a lever of control over your moods, and it is through self-starvation, which releases neurochemicals that make you feel high. While overeaters may get a jolt of pleasure from eating something with a flavor punch, your pleasure centers are disordered and seem to require malnutrition.

3. It is a dire necessity for adults to be loved, accepted, and approved of,

instead of the rational idea that adults do not have to get what they want, including love, respect, and acceptance. Rejection is just another's opinion of my worth, one with which I may gullibly agree or rationally disagree. My worth as a human being cannot be proven or disproven. I choose, therefore, to accept or love myself simply because it feels better than to dislike myself. In this matter, mine is the final word. (See idea 5, Chapter 6.) When people show concern that I am not eating enough, I am being treated as a child, and because I much prefer to be regarded as an adult, I will find other means than self-starvation on which to establish relationships with others.

And here is an irrational idea that is dedicated to thin ones:

4. I am powerless to eat food when I do not feel hungry,

instead of the rational idea that when I am malnourished, food is the equivalent of medicine, and as an adult I am quite capable of taking medicine that tastes bad.

5. Because I have committed certain acts, or behaved offensively, or harmed someone, I should moralistically blame and condemn myself,

instead of the rational idea that as a human being I am uniquely fallible. I may feel regret, remorse, or sadness for my behavior and mistakes, but I need not conclude that I am a worthless person. (See idea 7, Chapter 6.) There is nothing about having an eating disorder that proves I am worth less as a person, and when I am recovered from my disorder I will *not* have proven that I am any more worthwhile, either. Therefore I can take the elegant shortcut to self-acceptance right now by simply deciding to condemn myself no longer for anything at all. Instead, I will "make up" my self-worth out of thin air, because there is no good reason not to do so, because no one can stop me from doing it, because I will immediately feel better when I start accepting and valuing myself, and because my eating disorder will be much improved or even eliminated when I independently make my claim to unconditional self-acceptance.

It will be helpful to remember that anorexics are not a mysterious kind of people who can only be understood by others with the same problem or by people with "important letters" after their names. Although you have a serious problem that will require considerable effort to overcome, it will be much easier if you KISS (keep it simple, silly). That way, no matter what amount of intelligence you have, you will have enough of it to grasp the rational insights that can resolve your eating disorder. Read *Taming the Feast Beast*, attend RR-Fatness meetings if possible, and if you are unable to eat responsibly within several weeks, you would do well to see a professional therapist.

CHAPTER 9

Your Fatness Group

Having now read *Taming the Feast Beast,* you may, if you choose, consider yourself a participant in Rational Recovery. Just reading this book may be sufficient for you to overcome the philosophy of fatness that has been sustaining your body proportions and compulsive overeating for many years. However, it has been shown over and over that people often do better with self-help projects such as weight reduction in the company of similarly affected people. Naturally, if there is an RR-Fatness group in your area, plan to attend regularly for about a month or two, and then perhaps less frequently for the rest of your first year of recovery. Then you will have a good foundation for permanent weight control, and your recovery from the philosophy of fatness will probably be complete, even though you may not yet have attained your preferred weight. When you are doing well with weight control and would like to help others with Rational Recovery, you may be interested in being a coordinator for your present group or starting a new group closer to your home or on a different day of the week.

RR chemical dependency groups have flourished in the United States since RRS began its national programming in 1987. In the self-help network, advisers sometimes act as resource persons who are well known to the group and who can be called on when there are serious problems in the group that are beyond self-help. Coordinators, however, have a much more flexible role, and they act more as informal leaders or facilitators, as described in the next several pages.

Group formation can be handled entirely by an interested layperson who acts as an organizer—who pulls the group together and manages the details along the way. To express your interest in being appointed an organizer, just contact Rational Recovery Systems, Box 800, Lotus CA 95651 (916-621-2667 or 916-621-4374).

What Is an RR Meeting Like?

In the rational mode of recovery, you will learn to feel good and lose weight all on your own, without the necessity of outside help and without depending on other people or Higher Powers to help you out. You are ultimately alone in your struggle against your eating problems. Reading *Taming the Feast Beast* is an excellent way of informing yourself about self-inspired weight reduction.

In hundreds of communities, there are now Rational Recovery Systems self-help groups that meet once or twice per week, free of charge. One might ask, aren't people who go to these meetings getting outside help? Aren't they really depending on those groups for recovery?

Not really, because dependency is relative—a matter of degree, and a matter of convenience. The purpose of RR meetings is to accelerate the learning that is necessary for self-correction. While many people do this in the privacy of their own homes, and without reading books, the RR groups are excellent *resources* for people who want to work aggressively on weight control. Appearing at an RR meeting is better viewed as a powerful act of self-determination than as a sign of weakness or powerlessness.

Groups and meetings do not keep people thin or eating correctly; people do. The RR group is not a fellowship, nor is it a support group. There are no sponsors in RR, and when you do not appear at a meeting, people will likely assume that you are probably occupied with something better to do.

Naturally, people will tend to make friends with people they meet regularly and will have a tendency to hang around with people who are like-minded—a "rational crowd." This is encouraged in the rational mode of recovery, because it is often desirable to establish new social contacts while undertaking personal change. But RR members are cautioned against becoming emotionally dependent on personalities who appear at the meetings. Human beings, while they are delightful in many ways, are not to be trusted with your essential well-being. If you socialize with group members, you will probably find more appropriate topics of discussion than your own struggles with fatness.

If you do not understand something that is presented in an RR meeting—or in this book, for that matter—the fault is not yours, but the fault of the speaker or writer. This is in contrast to the "fake it till you make it" arrangement in traditional programs that assumes first of all that the program is true and that newcomers are ignorant of the truth. In RR, all questions are valid and deserve reasonable, plausible answers. Sometimes answers will take some time and effort to obtain; Rational Recovery can be hard work.

RR meetings have little structure, but there is certainly a weighty agenda. Meetings usually are started by the coordinator, who asks an overhead question such as "It's seven o'clock. Who's been having trouble eating correctly?" (Of course, everyone has, because that is why everybody is present.) Lively discussion may stem from that opener, but if everyone stays silent, a question may follow: "Then who has some question or some recent problem to talk about?"

In the ensuing *rational discussion,* the purpose is to discover the irrational foundations of relapse and emotional disturbance. As members speak, irrationalities will become evident to those listening. The purpose in eliciting this information is not to demonstrate how degenerate or helpless or powerless one is, but simply to give an example for discussion and learning. If someone has overeaten, or is showing weight gain, or is having trouble getting started with correct eating, the group assists that person with observations and input, *applying the principles of Rational Recovery.* The tools for RR group discussion are the Addictive Voice Recognition Technique (AVRT) and the ABC model of rational-emotive behavior therapy, both described in detail in this volume. Exotic dietary information, including information on vitamin therapy, fad diets, crash diets, fasting, pyramid power, bioenergetics, scientology, neurolinguistic programming, spiritual advice, meditational exercises, and exercise programs are all available elsewhere in most communities and are therefore inappropriate as topics in RR meetings. At RRS we have learned that people are usually quite capable of gathering together around a common problem, delving into that problem through study and discussion, and then using intelligence and reason to reach a solution to the problem.

Many RR groups suggest that members keep a Rational Spreadsheet on their laps, scanning the left column for irrational ideas as others speak. Then, at a good moment, anyone may interrupt to point out what that irrational idea was. Members usually use the ABC's of REBT to work through the irrationalities. Naturally, each person is also attempting to learn more about the addictive voice—the Feast Beast—that urges each member to overly nourish himself or herself. By listening for the Feast Beast in others, one may become more acutely aware of one's own addictive thinking. *Remember that the Feast Beast, or whatever caricature or metaphor is used for food-specific thinking, has only to do with ideas that support incorrect eating and does not refer to irrationalities in general.*

Members get together once or twice a week, talk sense about eating, impulse control, and personal problems, and go home until the next meeting. There are no sponsors, no weigh-ins, no confessions of past caloric sins, no lectures, no therapists, no steps, no sacred writings, and—other than donations—no fees. When *Taming the Feast Beast* is used as a discussion topic, it is to be regarded as an imperfect work subject to criticism, refutation, and revision. If individuals have trouble understanding the contents of *Taming the Feast Beast* it may be assumed that the deficiency lies in the book and not the reader. The RR program is largely contained in *Taming the Feast Beast;* therefore, some general consensus over the Rational Recovery philosophy is essential.

As you continue attending RR-Fatness meetings, you will become aware of other people's Beasts. This is therapeutic for you, because your own Beast is cleverly concealed within your own thoughts and often seems actually to be you. As you become more alert to other members' Beasts, you will "hear yourself" and discover your own endless variations on the theme of "Eat more now." RR meetings are sometimes like a game of hide-and-seek, where the Beast is rooted out of hiding. When it is found, the game is over and another one is started.

RR is training in emotional independence, so members are discouraged from abusing any new relationships that are formed at meetings. In other words, if you strike up a new friendship, you probably will not burden that person with your emotional disturbances between meetings. Instead, you will simply relapse or binge, if you wish, and then later tell the group about the irrational thinking that preceded your relapse.

Because overeating is often in response to some emotional upset, it is important to focus some of each meeting on the ABC's of REBT, as described in Chapters 4 and 6, and as described in the many informative and self-help books available from Lotus Press, Box 800, Lotus CA 95651.

Taking Strong Action

Sometimes people require an initial period of structure and intensive therapy in the principles of Addictive Voice Recognition Technique (AVRT) to establish stable patterns of correct eating. There is a growing number of licensed Rational Recovery centers in the United States, where one may learn Addictive Voice Recognition Technique. Persons with problems of food addiction, compulsive overeating, pronounced overweight conditions, or chronic relapse patterns may consider a residential stay at an RR service center. Residents are usually required to submit the results of a recent physical examination, and in some cases a medical treatment plan for weight loss and maintenance.

Meeting Notes
by Jack Trimpey, L.C.S.W; President, RRS

Having traveled over most of the country in the past several years, I have had the opportunity to sit in on hundreds of RR meetings in many locations. Personally, I get genuine pleasure in doing this, because I am seeing a growing society of rational people. That's good for everyone. As a relatively new self-help program, RR is doing nicely nationwide, with local projects flourishing in hundreds of cities in America, Australia, Japan, Canada, and Europe.

Each RR-Fatness group is a discussion and study group that focuses on *Taming the Feast Beast* and literature of the Institute for REBT. Participants talk openly about their difficulties with overeating and with negative emotions. These discussions lead naturally to broader issues of self-acceptance, anger toward others and self, guilt, family conflict, grudges, social anxieties, and problems with perfectionism and failure. *Occasionally* an adviser is present to provide direction and input, but normally the group is led by one of its members, a coordinator who likes explaining RR to others. The group finds its own way to some purposeful discussion relevant to overweight conditions, the addictive voice, and other related topics.

One problem that has cropped up in several groups is group dependency on structure and leadership. Since RR is based on the *independence* model of recovery rather than the "dependency training" model of traditional programs, structure and potent leadership are purposely kept to a minimum. For newcomers, this can be frustrating and sometimes even stressful. "What's this about?" and "What's going on?" are typical reactions in the leaderless and unstructured RR meetings. When these comments are accompanied by impatience or irritability, they may be recognized as signs of *emotional dependency.* The RR program is designed to orient new people quickly to the ground rules of RR participation and to identify the ways the more experienced members can help them work into the process. To make the group process more effective, I have prepared the following set of ground rules for all RR group participants. As you will see, no one has any obligation to anyone else in the group, but there are some good reasons to get the ball rolling as quickly as possible when the meeting gets started.

The ground rules for RR meetings are listed below, but persons interested in starting an RR group will do well to obtain the *Official Coordinators' Manual* of the Rational Recovery Self-Help Network (RRSN, Box 800, Lotus CA 95651).

Ground Rules for Rational Recovery Meetings

1. You are here to learn about yourself so you can feel good about yourself and moderate your food intake.

2. No one will pressure you to eat less, lose weight, or make any other decision for you. You are in the driver's seat, just as you always have been. We make decisions for ourselves, not for others.

3. You stand to benefit from telling the group about your current life problems and negative emotions, especially when you have been bingeing or struggling with hunger. RR is a plan for you to learn to say "no" to incorrect eating and make it stick, and to reduce or eliminate negative emotions that lead to the bingeing cycle. If you feel someone's story is getting too long, interrupt with a question or some feedback. Stick to the here and now, except when past experiences illustrate a point or have some relevance to today. Talk about your feelings; they are important to gaining personal discipline.

4. The meetings are confidential: "What is said here stays here."

5. Unless you have read and reread *Taming the Feast Beast* or related material available from Lotus Press, Box 800, Lotus CA 95651, you will have trouble making the most of your meetings.

6. You have a vested interest in the RR group; it is your path to weight control. Help with arrangements, promote it in the community, and don't let responsibilities pile up on one person. Volunteer to tend the answering

machine, take turns managing RRS materials, open up the place and lock it, clean up afterward, put up posters, run ads in the paper, speak to local professionals and officials, etc.

7. You are neither encouraged nor discouraged from socializing with group members between meetings. That's a private matter. There shall be no address or phone lists circulated at meetings, although one may be kept by an RRS coordinator. Names that are collected are the property of Rational Recovery and are not to be used for other purposes. There is no sponsor or buddy system.

8. Start each meeting with the overhead question, "Who's been having trouble eating correctly?" This will lead directly into an AVRT discussion. Apply the ABC's to emotional problems related to overeating. Relapsing is a normal part of recovery and a valuable opportunity to learn how to avoid future bingeing *if you will use the RR program.*

9. The RR-Fatness program is for people with weight problems and eating disorders. If there is sufficient interest, RRS may identify persons to start a SODA (SoDependence Awareness) group for people whose problems are not primarily with eating disorders—sexual hangups, "love addictions," gambling, "codependence," and other so-called addictions.

10. Outside observers are not in the interests of the group, even if well-meaning. Students, researchers, media people, and others who just want to "come and see" should be referred to RRS administration in California (916-621-4374).

11. If you think someone is having serious problems at a meeting (really depressed, suicidal, physically restless, seeing things, or incoherent), urge that person to see his or her doctor or contact the local mental health center.

12. The reverse side of the Rational Spreadsheet lists key irrational ideas that lead to most emotional disturbance

in human beings. Refer to this list during meetings to see if you can identify those irrational themes in what other people say. For example, if you believe a speaker believes he or she is a louse, then tell that person so and why. If you detect someone else's hostile blaming attitude, call attention to that. If you think someone is searching for nirvana, call him or her on it. Remember: You are attacking an idea, not the person holding it. Let others join the discussion. Naturally, when you talk, you will be eager to hear the same kind of feedback from the group. That's why you're there. People who are strongly motivated to get better fast usually *memorize* the Rational Spreadsheet list so that it becomes part of their thinking.

13. When you leave RRS, replace yourself, especially if you have been carrying any responsibility. If you believe you are ready to leave the group, tell the group ahead of time. Sometimes this brings up matters you have not considered before. To predict that someone else is likely to relapse or have serious problems in the future is against the spirit (excuse the expression) of Rational Recovery. A member's last meeting, when announced ahead of time, should convey a positive tone of encouragement, and one is always welcome to return to RR at any time.

Official copies of these ground rules, Rational Spreadsheets, and the *Official Coordinators' Manual,* are available from RRSN, Box 800, Lotus CA 95651.*

"DO YOU HAVE AN EATING PROBLEM TO WORK ON?"

As RRS grows in its role as the second influential party in the self-help arena, there is a growing struggle in some communities to

* Reprinted and revised from *The Journal of Rational Recovery* (March–April 1990).

adjust to our presence. Happily, most communities are able to welcome the rational mode of recovery and actively support our representatives in their efforts to make RR a viable self-help resource. But in some areas there is resentment that RRS is setting up shop, and occasionally there are incidents of direct interference in RR group activities.

One persistent problem that taxes the patience of group facilitators is the presence in the group of persons who are there to argue twelve-step or other irrational viewpoints on matters of recovery rather than to learn about REBT or AVRT. They sometimes imply or even state that RR is "wrong" or a "dangerous" program and that RR should mend its ways. When facilitators attempt to argue back or defend RR concepts, there may be verbal conflict and disruption, and if the facilitators permit the speakers to continue, precious meeting time is wasted on irrelevant material.

RRS strongly recommends the following approach when it seems that someone is present who is disinterested in applying RR to themselves, representing the interests of an outside organization, or selling something. First, the facilitator may ask the recalcitrant one, "Do you have an eating problem to work on this evening?" If the outsider says "no," then the facilitator may tell him or her or them, "This is a confidential meeting of Rational Recovery, and it is for people who want to work on their problems. Outside observers are not allowed. I'm sorry, but I must ask you to leave." The facilitator will accept only a "yes" or a "no" as an answer to the question "Do you have an addiction to work on?" If, for example, the outsider responds, "I have been doing well in OA for five years," then the facilitator may ask, "Is it your addiction to OA, then, that you want to work on? Some of us here have been in OA and have learned to get along fine without it." When the twelve-stepper declines this, as most probably will, then the invitation to leave will need little further explanation. Of course, it is entirely possible that the intruder may *accept* your invitation to work on the OA dependency or another addiction, and, since overcoming dependencies is what RR is all about, you may welcome aboard yet another person seeking happiness through personal independence.

In the unlikely event that this kind of situation develops in your RR group, you may find this approach to conflict resolution efficient and helpful.

The Role of the RR-Fatness Coordinator

RRS has an internal certification program whereby one may become a certified RRS coordinator or adviser. These credentials, Certified Rational Recovery Coordinator (CRRC), Certified Rational Recovery Specialist (CRRS), and Certified RR Educator (CRREd.), are not required to be fully active as an RRS volunteer. Many coordinators find little purpose in acquiring the RRS credentials, but many others are interested in the truth-in-advertising aspects of a credential that says "Rational Recovery spoken here." Employers, for example, are likely to seek out RRS-certified applicants when the religious quality of the twelve-step approach is finally established in courts of law. People working in RR-Residential programs (for chemical dependency *and* for eating disorders) will be required to be certified at the Certified Rational Recovery Therapist (CRRT) level. In 1992, regional training leading to RRS certification was put into effect, so that most people now have access to low-cost educational programs in the rational mode of recovery from chemical dependency and eating disorders.

Excellent related reading material on REBT is available from The Rational Recovery Catalog (Lotus Press). We often hear comments about books listed there. Unless people have a basic understanding of REBT as described in *Taming the Feast Beast,* they are unlikely to make the best of meetings. Even so, newcomers are often able to get involved in the discussion right away, because rational ideas make such good sense from the start. Rational Recovery is based on the assumption that human beings, motivated out of self-interest, are quite capable of gathering together around a common problem and working on it constructively. RRS provides the conditions and materials that allow that to happen.

While others may choose a course of endless recovery and dependence on Higher Powers, RRS provides a fine means to break the chains of fatness independently and without undergoing a personal identity change. We ask of new members that they come with a critical attitude but be willing to use their intelligence to find faults in their own thinking. We also ask that they inform the group ahead of time when they intend to leave the group. It does take intelligence to participate in RR, but whatever amount of intelligence one has is always enough, as long as the individual *uses* it.

REBT is a type of psychotherapy that is taught in most universities, but there is also a self-help version of REBT that can be understood and used by anyone. REBT self-help is so simple and so effective in solving personal problems that it has often been called "uncommon sense." One example of REBT self-help is "Sticks and stones may break my bones, but names will never hurt me." Another example is "No use crying over spilt milk."

In Rational Recovery, we learn the "ABC's," which is the method of analyzing and evaluating our own thinking, especially our ideas about overeating and weight control. There is a standard, formal way to do this, and the Rational Spreadsheet is a worksheet that helps get our thinking down in black-and-white so we may dispute our own irrational ideas. Although doing ABC's is an important part of learning the RR program, AVRT is the heart of the program. It is important that the meetings be flexible, without any rigid format.

One of the coordinator's roles during meetings is simply to point out that certain ideas that are being expressed in the discussion are irrational, to explain why, and then to offer a rational concept as a better alternative. The best way to do this is by asking questions of a person who holds an irrational idea. For example, if I hear someone saying that it is hard to say "no" when offered a snack at a party, I assume that he or she irrationally believes that other people's opinions are extremely important and that he or she needs the acceptance or approval of others to feel well. I wouldn't get very far by saying, "You think that you need everyone's approval and you have to get rid of that false idea." But I would probably do better by *asking,* "What would happen if you refused to eat a snack at the party?" Then the member might level and say, "Everyone would think I'm weird and wonder what's wrong with me." Then I can ask another good question, "Why is it so important what those people think of you?" Now we are closer to finding this person's *shithood,* or the negative self-concept that leads one to *depend on the opinions of others* to define one's worth as a human being. With further discussion, the coordinator or someone else may offer the idea that it doesn't matter if other people like you, as long as you like yourself, and that can help the group focus on the rational idea of unconditional self-acceptance. This can be done without any discussion of ABC's, and no one has to have a Ph.D. or an M.S.W. to help out. This is really simple stuff and, as Dr. Albert Ellis has said many times, "Anyone can do it."

The job of a coordinator is to set the stage for open and honest discussion so that rational insights can be learned. If the coordinator knows the contents of *Taming the Feast Beast* reasonably well, he or she will have enough knowledge of AVRT and REBT to give the group discussion meaning and direction. The coordinator needs to be kind, considerate, and calm when working with others, but at the same time firm and assertive in pointing out the errors in others' thinking.

Coordinators should be careful not to take on the role of counselor or therapist, not only because that would be dishonest but also because that kind of role-playing feeds right into the *dependency* problems that most newcomers will have.

Although RR meetings may have little structure, we strive to give our *thinking* structure and to live an unpredictable, chancy life without eating incorrectly. Houses may burn, relationships may fall apart, jobs may be lost, and other serious misfortune may occur, but we remain calmly in control of ourselves through rational insights learned from readings and in group discussions. Instead of predictable ritual and dogma, our meetings help members form an intellectual strategy for getting the most out of life, focusing on the realities of day-to-day living. This strategy for correct eating is based on objective information that can be read, told to others, discussed, argued about, and understood.

RRS coordinators usually welcome the opportunity to be a leader in a revolutionary self-help movement and to participate in this important work of social change. Some of our best resources are the RRS advisers, qualified professionals in our communities who are committed to seeing change in the field of eating disorders. They can teach coordinators about the helping process and help when special problems crop up during group meetings.

It is easy for a "food-dependent" person to become dependent on others, especially on you. Dependency seems to be common to all groups, not just "food-dependent" people, and because of this, RRS advisers usually keep a cordial distance from the groups they advise. While dependence is encouraged and even taught and required in traditional programs, RR actively discourages dependency whenever possible. Coordinators do not advise or make decisions for others and are not responsible for how others eat, live, or die. What others do with their lives is their own choice; in RR, none of us is the other's keeper.

The only qualifications to be an RR coordinator are an understanding of how to help others become more rational, an understanding of the limitations of self-help, and the desire to be a coordinator.

So You'd Like to Have RR in Your Town!

We at RRS central offices in California have the privilege of speaking to many wonderful people who offer an endless stream of creativity to Rational Recovery Systems. Here are some local organizing ideas we have compiled:

- To get the ball rolling, find other people who are interested in helping. This immediately multiplies your efforts and increases the possibilities for developing the rational counterpoint. If you are a professional with an advanced degree in a field related to education or health care (teacher, social worker, nurse, doctor, clinical psychologist), you are qualified to become an adviser to an RR group. An adviser is a voluntary member who acts in an advisory way to a group.

- Coordinators have a natural ability to understand and explain the RR program to newcomers and to provide Rational Recovery in their communities. Coordinators are valuable people indeed! They are natural helpers who open doors for RRS and organize groups according to "instinct." It's difficult to make a mistake because so much of what RRS stands for is closely related to common sense.

- Another natural information source is your local library. A library, after all, is the central information resource for the community. A book that is often requested will be ordered by the Purchasing Department. Tell the librarian to order several copies of *Taming the Feast Beast* because it is used in a new self-help movement. Check back in a few weeks to find the status of the order.

- Individual members may post informational posters or cards in grocery stores, Laundromats, and public kiosks advertising what, where, and when RR is. Newspapers often have a community events calendar where meeting information can be posted. The best advertising is had by getting a life-style reporter from your local newspaper to write a local article. (Religion writers invariably do poorly for RRS, sensationalizing many of our members' independence from religious dogma.)

- Your chamber of commerce can often provide names and phone numbers of organizations to which RR information can be given. The United Way also often provides an information and referral service such as this.

- If you will provide RRS with a list of Zip codes within driving distance of your meeting place, we can generate letters and send them to persons whose names are in our data base, informing them that you desire to start an RR group, providing them with your name and phone number, and requesting their assistance and involvement.

- Obvious places for meetings include churches, libraries, and community service buildings. Not so obvious places include after-hours business locations such as beauty parlors, medical offices, bank boardrooms, or industrial complex meeting rooms. Since RR meetings are free, it is best to find a free meeting place; many organizations are willing to help with this. RRSN is a nonprofit educational organization, and we can provide you with a federal ID number if it is required for a meeting room.

- Although RR meetings are without charge, any incurred expenses should be absorbed by the group participants. It is important that coordinators avoid "going into the hole" to help others. Each group is financially autonomous but does not accept direct funding from organizations. For a group to function it is necessary to "pass the hat" to reimburse for phone calls, photocopying, advertising, or any other documented costs. A little notebook account should be kept and be open for anyone to see. Coordinators' and advisers' mileage is tax-deductible, since RR is nonprofit and since these positions are voluntary.

- Discounts on books are offered by Delacorte Press (1-800-223-6834; ask for Special Sales) to coordinators and advisers on orders of six or more books. The books are sold to group members at the retail price plus something toward the postage and handling charge, and the monetary difference is applied toward group expenses.

- Read *The Journal of Rational Recovery* to keep up-to-date on the social, clinical, and political issues. Encourage people to return the confidential questionnaire at the back of *Taming the Feast Beast,* since ongoing study is based on this information.

- You are one of the important links in this rapidly expanding coalition of people who are stepping forward to advocate for a large disenfranchised populace. And just remember: If you're not having fun doing it, you're not doing it right!

My Newfound Friend

My newfound friend is hunger
He daily walks with me.
Companion, joy, and comfort and
Encouragement is he,
He signals me his presence,
Activates the voice within.
Then self and voice have dialogue
Now self does always win.
Hunger tells me I'm victorious
Over the BEAST that used to rule.
The BEAST, in vain he still does fight;
I tell you he's no fool.
My BEAST waits patiently his turn.
He's always on the prowl.
He counts on those who still do yearn
For "bad foods"—oh, so foul.
But hunger smiles assuringly
And leads me by my head
To keep resolves for better health.
My banquet table's spread
With thoughts of things I want to do
And places not yet seen.
And visions of accomplishment
That I, from life, may glean.
Awakened hope, abundant joy
As I take this life in stride.
In my new self in truth I say
It's great to be alive!
—Phyllis Ludwig-Zillmann
RRSN, Florida

APPENDIX A

CONFIDENTIAL QUESTIONNAIRE

Rational Recovery Systems is conducting social research on self-help. Please forward this response to RRS, Box 800, Lotus CA 95651.

Name: Age: Sex:

Address:

Education:

Occupation:

Which term best describes your personal philosophy? (Christian, agnostic, atheist, humanist, Jew, Buddhist, etc.)

Weight upon receipt of *Taming the Feast Beast?*

_____lbs. Date:_____

Present weight?   Date:

Age of onset of overweight:

Presently losing, maintaining, gaining?

If now maintaining your desired weight, how long?

Previous cycles of weight gain and loss (dates and weights):

Have you attended RR meetings?

Did you or do you attend OA meetings?

How many/How long?

If you discontinued OA, why?

Other weight loss plans, programs, systems, fads, etc.:

Summarize your means for managing your weight problem:*

Evaluate the plan in *Taming the Feast Beast*:*

Appendixes B and C, which follow, are included because of their relevance to many readers. They are not included as part of the main text because, for the majority of readers, they are not directly related to the condition of fatness.

---

* You may use separate paper for any of these items.

APPENDIX B

DISCUSSION OF THE TWELVE-STEP APPROACH

The following monograph is based on the chapter titled "A Discussion of the Twelve-Step Spiritual Healing Program of Alcoholics Anonymous" in *The Small Book,* 4th ed., by Jack Trimpey, L.C.S.W. (Delacorte Press, 1992). In its original form, the subject under discussion was alcohol dependence, and the purpose was to vindicate the millions of chemically dependent people who are forced into religious indoctrination by the absence of any alternative. The reality is somewhat different in the field of weight control and weight reduction because of the presence in most communities of several options for persons with eating disorders. Even so, twelve-step programs are still one of the most widespread and influential programs of self-help and institutional care throughout the nation. Consequently, many overweight persons who are ill suited for the spiritual healing approach find themselves participating in OA. Therefore, the following discussion is offered as reading for individuals who have attended OA and may still have residual ideas of dependency and powerlessness resulting from that exposure to twelve-stepism. The parallels between AA and OA aren't perfect, but the general points of discussion seem to fit well enough to warrant publication here.

Following is a story of "Sara," who had an unfortunate experience in OA. After her story, you may explore an examination of the twelve-step program as it applies to overeating, and then some common assumptions about eating disorders that have their origins in the disease model of the twelve-step program.

SARA

I had just lost my job as an administrative assistant in an ambitious company, and I was left with more idle time than I had had for years. Being a professional woman, I took pride in my appearance, and I don't mind saying that I was good-looking. My job always came before men, and I had figured that eventually I would marry when my finances were in better shape. Lots of guys would pay attention to me when I dressed the part, and I could have a date without effort. At home and jobless, though, I was literally out of circulation with my old office contacts, and no one called. Worse yet, I had trouble finding a job I was qualified for and interested in, so I began to feel trapped, like I was out of control of my life. I began to have frequent snacks, and when I would take walks alone, I would stop at junk food stands and ice cream parlors and pig out. I started watching more TV than before, always with some munchies at my side, and even my taste in TV viewing sank to new lows—games, soaps, and sitcom reruns. Within two months I had hit 140 pounds, and that really gave me a jar. I looked at myself in the mirror while drying off after a shower and felt really put off and ugly. "You're fat. Fat and ugly—that's you." I energized myself, got a couple of diet books at the drugstore, and resolved I would not let myself go like that ever again.

I started by getting rid of all the junk food, butter, and mayo, and I bought mostly veggies. During my first week of dieting, I lost five pounds! I felt great, but only temporarily. "But I'm still fat. There're still fifteen pounds to go. At the present rate, that'll take at least another month, but actually it'll take much longer, because the first five pounds are the easiest." I remember feeling uneasy about the challenge of losing those fifteen pounds, but I didn't dwell on it. But the next day, I bought a carton of cheese Danishes, came home, and inside of three hours finished off all six of them. They were wonderful, and I felt horrible. I hadn't done that for a month, and now I'd blown it. "Oh, well," I thought, "nobody's perfect, and tomorrow's another day." So, before tomorrow came, I went around the corner and had a double cheeseburger, a chocolate malt, and a medium fries.

When tomorrow did finally arrive, I awoke and felt numb. I could feel my belly in rolls I hadn't noticed before, and I had visions of the previous afternoon and evening, with me pigging out on all that forbidden food. I went to the bathroom and weighed myself, and I had gained back three pounds. "A whole month of discipline and I'm only down two pounds. That diet sure is shot to hell. Right now, it just isn't worth it. There's no use torturing yourself, Sara. You have too many things to worry about without all this diet stuff, and besides, you don't look all that *bad." So out the window went the diet, and in the door came all the butter, pasta, meat, candy, cookies, and beloved mayo.*

I continued to look for a job a little each day, but my dresses, the really snazzy job-hunting ones, were pulling here and there. When I saw myself in the mirror, I would get a cold feeling inside, and finally I decided that I would have to invest some of my cash reserve in a new job-hunting wardrobe. I got two conservative, loose-fitting, drapy things to cover my increasingly unhappy 155 pounds.

I began to hate myself for being fat, and I imagined getting a surprise visit from someone at the office I used to date who had lost my home phone number. I imagined him coming in and looking shocked and sorry for me, and avoiding any touching or closeness and just talking about the way things used to be and then hurrying off without asking for my phone number. When I would visit my parents, we would be in a fury in no time, because my mother was also worried about my weight gain and kept asking personal questions and making suggestions, such as seeing a doctor or trying the special diet that helped Uncle Carl lose forty-one pounds. I finally withdrew from seeing my parents and went out of my apartment just once a day to go through the motions of getting a newspaper for the job section and picking up the only real comfort I knew, more goodies. I slept longer, let the house get messier, and got fatter and fatter as the weeks wore on.

Just above the job section one day, I noticed a tiny ad for "Overeaters Anonymous," and I called the number immediately. There was only a taped message, but it gave the time and place for a meeting, and I was there that evening. In the recreation hall basement, I met people of all sizes, mostly fat like me or fatter, and it seemed that I had found a happy home where I could get my act together. Overeaters Anonymous is a plan in which people help each other to control their eating, a group of closely knit people who study a system of self-improvement called the twelve steps. Some talked about the amazing problems they had with overeating, and others talked about how they had used the group as a support in losing weight. In looking at their figures, I thought I could tell how long they had been coming by their size, but I was wrong. Some of the fattest ones had been coming for many years, and some of the normal-sized ones had been attending only a short time.

"Never say die," I thought. They gave me some materials describing the twelve-step program, and when I looked them over I knew immediately that it wasn't for me. I decided to stay in the group, however, because I know very well how to ignore people's religious talk and still get some good out of relationships with them. I knew I wanted to lose weight, and I was assured that "There's room for all degrees of disbelief, and you may take what you like and leave the rest. All that is necessary is a sincere desire to eat less and lose weight."

I didn't much like having a sponsor who was interested in what I ate, but I knew that all I had tried hadn't worked and these people were more experienced than I. It worried me that my sponsor was heavier than I, but she explained that the program has a different meaning to each person there, and her weight would vary like anyone else's and then decline. "I am not an example," she said, "but only one who cares about you. By caring for you I am helped, and that's how the program works." I accepted this sponsor, actually a pleasant person who reminded me of my mother years before, and between meetings we would talk on the phone about many things, including my appetite, urges to eat, and cravings.

At the meetings I often felt I was telling more about myself than was relevant to losing weight, but the group had an endless appetite for anything I had to say about myself. At the end of two months of OA meetings and many talks with my sponsor, I had lost all of four pounds. The group thought that was wonderful, but I didn't. "Two pounds per month is not good enough," I told my sponsor after the *group meeting. "At my present 175 pounds, it will take two years to reach my goal. I can't afford that kind of time."*

"We can't hurry God in these matters," she said, "and you have the rest of your life to find your peace in your Higher Power. You see my present weight, and it has been there for many years. I'm learning my serenity now, and the weight loss will come soon enough for me. It will come to you, too, Sara."

"But Brenda," I said, "I don't believe in any Higher Power. I want to lose weight, and that's all OA asks for, isn't it? Just a sincere desire?"

"That's enough to get started, but there's more to it. We are powerless and will always be personally powerless to control our overeating. That is why we all must rely on something more powerful than ourselves. I know you haven't really been working the steps like you should, but I know that for many it takes time. Have you prayed for help with this?"

For the first time, I realized that I was being drawn into something I did not really agree with. I was unable really to ignore the spiritual teachings of OA because there is nothing else offered in place of the twelve steps as they are written. I do remember that there would be many attempts to make common sense of the religious steps, like the part when they say, "Anything can be your Higher Power—even a doorknob." To this I just laughed and said, "How interesting, but— no, thank you." In other words, I had come to OA to lose weight, but the only means provided to do so is to form dependencies on a Higher Power and other people and plan to keep coming to meetings forever. I told Brenda I would probably stop coming to meetings, and I expected that she would understand and remain a friend, but she said, "It is unlikely that you will get better from your overeating unless you find your Higher Power. I will be here if and when you decide to come back."

Quitting OA was a taste of defeat, but I knew I was better off on my own. I struggled for a few more months until finally I saw another ad, in the Sacramento Bee, *for Rational Recovery. I called the number and talked to Jack Trimpey, but I was disappointed to learn that RR was only for alcoholics. I asked Jack if RR would also work with overeaters, and he said that it certainly could, but there would have to be some minor changes with the Beast concept. I really had no idea what he was talking about, but he sent me a copy of* The Small Book.

In one evening of reading The Small Book *I overcame a lifetime of prejudice against myself and I can see clearly that my problem was not overeating, or overweight, or anything else but the idea that my worth to myself varies along with my weight—that each mark on the scale of pounds translated into a score of human worth. Realizing this took the sense of urgency out of losing weight and I found that I was able to focus on eating correctly rather than on each ounce of body weight I lost or gained. I don't think that my improvement in self-esteem would have been enough to change my eating habits, because they were so ingrained. As a matter of fact, I had already toyed with the idea of just accepting myself as a fat person, "pleasingly plump," and giving up on weight reduction. But the Beast concept, AVRT (explained fully in Chapters 4 and 5 of* Taming the Feast Beast*) fits in perfectly with the self-esteem concepts of REBT, and I have found it much easier to say "no" to food than I ever thought possible. My weight is now falling, never as fast as I would like, but weight loss is no longer the center of my life. I have taken a part-time job at a department store while I continue to look for a better position in my chosen field, and I am building a circle of friends who aren't really interested in food, dieting, and overweight. But I am losing weight by controlling my own thoughts about eating, so I'll also take the credit, thank you. [Sara is a composite of several women known to the authors.—L.T.]*

Because the need for a rational alternative that avoids the faddism of most diet books, the fees of diet centers and pill programs, and farfetchedness of the twelve-step program, the following discussion is included in *Taming the Feast Beast.* It is not the purpose here to persuade OA members or devout theists that their views are wrong, or to discredit the successes of programs that many have found helpful. Instead, we will simply examine each of the steps of OA from the perspective of an inquiring mind, asking the questions that will come naturally to anyone who is not already convinced of the overall correctness of the twelve-step creed.

As you read this short critique of the twelve steps, you will notice that taken together they comprise a philosophy in which one is powerless, submissive to authority, unequipped to function independently, and in endless need of external support and guidance. This should not be surprising to anyone, and to take offense that this is pointed out would seem to deny the reality of twelve stepism. The twelve steps are derived from an ancient philosophy with which we are all familiar. Like it or not, the ideas below reflect the philosophical underpinnings of American society. They have often been held up as an ideal for the entire world. For our purposes they are a philosophy of fatness.

Step 1: *"We admitted we were powerless over our addictions—that our lives had become unmanageable."*

Step 1 actually teaches overeaters that they are not responsible for what they put in their mouths, that they have no capacity to refrain from overeating. Could it be that compulsive overeating is largely a *result* of this idea? That is, isn't the overeater already expressing the idea that his or her desire for large amounts of fattening food is an absolute need, that a craving is irresistible or intolerable, and that, when the desire to eat occurs, it must be gratified immediately and completely? To the extent that this is so, the message in this first step could be counterproductive to those who are concerned enough to attend a few meetings of OA but not really inclined to adopt the social or theological elements of OA spiritualism.

Learned helplessness from Step 1 often can be a self-fulfilling prophecy in which the addict retains this central spiritual principle of surrender even after quitting OA. For example, after attending a few meetings you may decide that OA isn't for you, that you can slim down or lose weight on your own. So you stop attending meetings, determined to eat less and lose weight on your own. However, something lingers in your thinking, and it won't go away. When you are on the verge of a binge, you think back to what was said at the OA meetings, and you remember the sincere people and their stern warnings:

You are powerless over food and you have no control; only a Higher Power can restore you to sanity. We all tried it on our own, and none of us could eat sanely until we found our Higher Power. You can't resist the overpowering urge to eat, and if you leave this group you will binge again; then it's all downhill. This group is a lifeboat; leave us and you'll sink. There's no escape except through our loving God, Who gives us the strength to abstain, one day at a time.

This kind of indoctrination does *nothing* to help your resolve not to binge; it is probably *the worst thing* to tell someone who is having problems with impulse control and who does not believe in a *rescuing* deity. If you are seriously tempted to overeat and all those experienced people say you're powerless to resist, who are *you* to argue the point? "Down the hatch—cheers!" Your weight gain is highly predictable.

The chief problem with the idea of powerlessness, even greater than the negative psychological impact it has on overeaters, is its utter falsity. There are simply too many examples of overeaters, including these writers (J.T. and L.T.), who "wise up and slim down" when the consequences of being overweight become too costly, too distasteful, too risky, or too painful. Self-initiated weight loss is extremely common, and practically everyone knows someone who was formerly overweight, then chose to eat correctly, and is now maintaining a desirable weight. We have encountered many such people in our personal and professional lives who have lost weight and kept it off without *any* program or reliance on Higher Powers. It is doubtful that any of us could have helped ourselves if we were really convinced of the truth of Step 1. Large numbers of people find within themselves the ability to lose weight and eat correctly, and many others achieve their goal of weight loss and correct eating by getting professional help or attending other weight loss programs. The charge that when an overeater seeks help for his or her problem he or she is admitting powerlessness is simply not true. Reaching out for help is in itself a powerful act of self-determination; *your life isn't unmanageable!*

Step 2: *"We came to believe that a Power greater than ourselves could restore us to sanity."*

It should be noted that *The Big Book* of Alcoholics Anonymous is the central document of all twelve-step programs, and its influence on thinking about overeating is pervasive and profound. It was written by the founders of AA over fifty years ago, by two men who attained sobriety following the Christian plan of salvation. Several of their contemporaries, members of "The Oxford Group," attempted earlier to found a sect of recovering alcoholics based on a more orthodox interpretation of Christian theology that emulated first-century Christianity. They failed, partly because of the explicit religious dogma they sought to incorporate, leaving the "Akron Group," with its ambiguous "Higher Power," to evolve into the dominant theistic organization it is today. *The Big Book,* about two inches thick, devotes an entire derisive chapter to "agnostics."

It is important to address *The Big Book's* aspersions on humanists, atheists, agnostics, skeptics, "disbelievers," and those whose personal views do not include a *rescuing* deity. "Twelve-step bashing" (a euphemism for "blasphemy!") isn't our purpose in challenging *The Big Book;* our concern is for the desperate persons who are harmed by its dogmatic stance. The twelve-step program is a *direct attack* on the nonreligious groups listed above. With our constitutional guarantees, all's fair in the discourse between religionists and nonreligionists, but little attention is paid to the intellectual violence done to sick people who do not endorse God, Jesus, the Bible, Christianity, or religion in general, or to religious people who do not endorse OA's "spiritual" teachings. One purpose of *Taming the Feast Beast* is to vindicate those individuals—to ensure that each person, regardless of personal philosophy, has a maximum opportunity to overcome eating disorders at the self-help level of action.

Major problems develop when a weight loss program relies on divine intervention, or what is commonly called "faith healing." Simply put, people must *make* themselves *believe* in a Higher Power because there is no objective evidence that such a Higher Power exists. For many people making believe this way comes easily, while others find it virtually impossible. It is such a being, a benevolent, rescuing deity called "God as you understand Him," on which OA rests.

"But," the OA elders insist, "there is room for all degrees of disbelief in OA. Anything can be your Higher Power! Your HP can be a wrench, a tree, music, the OA group, even Wisdom, but you absolutely *must* place your faith in something greater than, and outside of, yourself."

This tactic is, in a word, unethical. It is practiced everywhere in the twelve-step spiritual network and obviously has the sanction of its leaders. This is a cultish tactic that, in the view of many, detracts from the dignity and credibility of the twelve-step program. It's a bait-and-switch head game in which the real intention is to convert a neophyte to hard-core belief in God Almighty. Suppose a doubting newcomer accepts a doorknob as his Higher Power on the advice of well-intentioned members. Granted, he or she may ignore impulses to eat while meditating on the finer dimensions of the doorknob, but what about the next hurdle, Step 3?

Step 3: *"We made a decision to turn our will and our lives over to the care of God, as we understand Him."*

Ah, now—it isn't the doorknob, is it? Now our newcomer is faced with the task of reconciling his newfound control with a new, poorly understood "God." Bye-bye, doorknob. Maybe it's time for a double hamburger.

The Higher Power of OA is a flexible "training deity" devised to (1) help neophytes distract themselves from impulses and appetites, (2) avoid disclosing the inflexible theism behind OA, and (3) provide a progressive relaxation of critical judgment so neophytes can be further indoctrinated in OA theology. Notice that there is still equivocation with ". . . as we understand Him." Even though "He" rates a capital letter, you are led to believe that you are still at liberty to make "Him" what you believe "Him" to be. Sure you are.

Step 4: *"We made a searching and fearless moral inventory of ourselves."*

Here we find that recovering fat people are expected to become better people. Is adult life really a struggle to "be good"? Come on, now. If some folks define adult life that way, then fine for them, but it would seem that there are far better reasons for seeking weight loss than to "be a good person." We find here also the pernicious idea that "good" people are less likely to be overweight than less "moral" people. Why should an overeater be required to search introspectively for "moral defects" in himself or herself? (Good people, of course, never get fat.) Are diabetics similarly obliged to make searching and fearless moral inventories? If not, why not? If an overeater loses weight but still robs banks, was the treatment successful? Of course it was!

The Christian roots of OA are most conspicuous here, where the neophyte is required to debase himself, to grasp downward at "humility" as an avenue to spiritual redemption through faith. "We are all sinners" supposedly gives way to moral ascendancy and the "miracle" of weight loss.

Step 4 presents difficulties for many disturbed persons whose defenses against self-condemnation are poor. There is speculation that persons are most prone to suicide or self-destructive relapses during this phase of OA indoctrination, when the inductee is flooded with conditioned guilt and remorse and is unable to stem the tide of his or her self-condemnation. Unfortunately, data regarding this problem are scarce because of OA's lack of accountability and disdain for keeping records of persons experiencing such difficulties. Keep in mind that most of OA group activity occurs in church basements and social halls under lay leadership (the strongest ego dominates the meetings), and few persons served by OA ever come to the attention of professional caregivers. *The Big Book* does give a vivid example of an individual who did commit suicide while trying unsuccessfully to "get his Higher Power together," and the writer describes this incident almost cavalierly as *something to be expected when one fails the test of faith*—that is, "The wages of sin is death." This all gets very, very Christian, which is fine for many Christians, but wouldn't an inventory (list) of irrational ideas that perpetuate the bingeing cycle be more appropriate in most cases?

Step 5: *"We admitted to God, to ourselves, and to another human being the exact nature of our wrongs."*

The idea here is that by confessing our sins, the listener will forgive (accept) us in spite of our having committed the misdeed. Forgiving is the opposite of blaming (or condemning) someone for committing an antisocial, degenerate, or other unacceptable act. Forgiveness by God is a temporary antidote for guilt because its message is, "God says you are still a good person even though you acted badly, and who are you to question the opinion of God?"

At this point we come to the OA sponsor system. Briefly, it is a "buddy system" of interpersonal dependency wherein the neophyte "borrows the ego" of a program veteran and attempts to identify with one who has "been through it." There are many inspiring stories about how a faltering neophyte called his or her sponsor in the wee hours and found strength and encouragement to resist the temptation to binge. I have also spoken with overeaters who believe that their dependency on a sponsor was unwarranted (considering that sponsors have no special training or skills) and overeaters whose emotional entanglement with a sponsor led to serious problems. While there will probably be occasional abuses in any kind of human relationship, it is worth pointing out here that emotional dependency among normal adults is categorically self-defeating, even when one party is deemed the helper. The sponsor system clearly encourages the irrational idea that one *needs* someone other or greater than oneself on whom to rely.

Sponsors hear confession from neophytes with the understanding that confession is intrinsically beneficial and healing. This assumption is contradicted by the fact that confession programs are interminable, open-ended affairs in which the confessor never attains personal liberation from guilt, from the philosophy of guilt, or from the confession ritual. In OA, God listens to and forgives confessions eternally. In Rational Recovery, individuals confess nothing; instead, they learn to accept themselves as imperfect yet worthy beings who seek only self-forgiveness and who reject guilt as a matter of principle. Self-disclosure, then, is simply a means of identifying problem areas for self-improvement.

Step 6: *"We were entirely ready to have God remove all these defects of character."*

It is probably difficult for religious persons to imagine why this idea is so offensive to some people who are not religious, but I will attempt to explain anyway. What is being asked for in Step 6 is a miracle. Members must believe that miracles are possible and theirs for the asking. Accepting the miracles of slimness, survival, and serenity from a Higher Power while other group members fail to qualify for miracles is thought to be character-building. In Step 5 there is some connection between what the neophyte is being asked to do and a potential benefit. If you confess, you may be forgiven, and that may help somewhat. But now the neophyte is being asked to get ready for a miracle—*entirely* ready. Well, suppose he or she is only partly ready? Or almost ready? Would this rescuing deity hold out on a sincere person who is not entirely ready? Is "entirely" inserted to cover for when the rescuing deity, in His infinite wisdom, doesn't come through with the desired character repairs? Why did this rescuing deity endow us with fat bodies in the first place—just to stir up a little trouble? So He could show off later with character repairs? To test our mettle? To lead us to OA?

The "wrongs," or mistakes, or misdeeds that one confessed to in Step 5 (after the "fearless moral inventory" of Step 4) have now been converted to "defects of character," which are to be removed through divine intervention after some additional qualifying "steps."

Step 7: *"We humbly asked Him to remove these shortcomings."*
Any priest or minister will immediately recognize here the setting of "a proper worshipful attitude" that is a requisite for prayer and ritual. We do not firmly or politely request favors from the deity, nor do we expect a decent response to a request we think would be just and fair unless we humbly submit ourselves to the Lord, unworthy as we are, in the hope that our pleas for mercy and favor will not be dismissed or ignored. It is to escape precisely this kind of groveling and self-debasement that many people flee from churches. It is in this step that we learn that in OA weight loss is a supernatural miracle, not really the product of our own

self-determination. Is it really character-building to believe that our well-being is subject to the whims of a rescuing deity?

A curious thing about the twelve steps is that not a single word is said about the means to eat correctly, nor is there any suggestion as to how an overeater might arrive at a decision to eat correctly. The idea of personal choice is absent. The program simply assumes that by becoming morally good, people will overcome their eating disorders. Conversely, fatness is viewed as a clear moral failure, as separation from God, as a spiritual deficit to be remedied by a "spiritual awakening," that is, religious conversion.

Step 8: *"We made a list of all the persons we had harmed, and became willing to make amends to them all."*

A list? Became willing? Something's cooking here.

Step 9: *"We made direct amends to such people wherever possible, except when to do so would injure them or others."*

"I feel so guilty, I can't live with myself. I *need* your approving opinions. Please respect me. Don't blame me for being bad. Help me feel better. Forgive me. I want to be good."

Freud and others have written about the common defense mechanism of "undoing," wherein guilt-flooded persons seek to compensate for earlier misdeeds by symbolically or actually acting out scenarios that absolve the offense. To the extent that Steps 8 and 9 are to absolve persistent guilt about past misdeeds or culinary "sins," wouldn't self-forgiveness be more appropriate than dwelling on past mistakes and possibly opening old wounds? Don't decent people apologize? Isn't simply losing weight enough? Aren't Steps 8 and 9 melodramatic and cloying? Are they really relevant to one's appetite disorder? Are these steps intended to help others, or are they stairsteps of moral ascendancy?

Step 10: *"We continued to take personal inventory and when we were wrong promptly admitted it."*

Here we find out that OA is forever, cradle to grave. The program is interminable; members continue—and continue and continue and continue—year after year, decade after decade, to take searching and fearless moral inventories and they promptly admit when they are wrong, unless, of course, the error is said to lie in the twelve-step program. The idea of leaving the fold, leaving Mother Group, is anathema to OA. Members dwell on stories of those who "tried it on their own" only to binge again, and then, when the weight has been regained or some worse consequence occurred, came crawling back to old Mother Group. Occasionally mention is made of so-and-so, who left ten years ago and lost weight independently, but "She can't really be happy, we know she's really miserable, she'll never keep the weight off. . . ." The message of personal powerlessness is so strong that it becomes a self-fulfilling prophecy. Those who quit OA are likely to remember the grim pronouncements that those who leave the group are surely doomed. Then, in a moment of indecision, they succumb to the "inevitable" and resume their patterns of gluttony.

Doesn't almost everyone, except possibly some sociopathic or mentally ill people, try to "be good"? Aren't people who try to lose weight already trying to "be good"? Are overeaters so morally defective as to need constant indoctrination, constant and repeated FMI's (fearless moral inventories)? Does Step 10, with its insistence that life is a constant struggle to maintain one's desired weight and morality, contribute to self-doubt rather than a healthy sense of assumed personal competence and goodness? Doesn't Step 10 really reflect the idea that life is only a stage for endless conflict between the pervasive forces of good and evil?

Step 11: *"We sought through prayer and meditation to improve our conscious contact with God as we understand Him, praying only for knowledge of His will and the power to carry that out."*

Each member is expected to become an agent of God, praying for instructions from on high and for the strength to carry out those instructions. OA adherents achieve a state of bliss, or inner peace, through meditation and prayer, a state they call "serenity," which is actually salvation through faith; this serenity is a major goal in the earthly lives of compulsive overeaters. Serenity, the peace that passeth all understanding, is regarded as a powerful hedge against overeating relapse. The phrase ". . . as we understand Him" is repeated, but by now it is clear that the deity in question is highly specific, One who sends messages and Who expects worship, prayer, meditation, and obedience as conditions to be met before character repairs are to be made. Wouldn't ". . . as OA understands Him" be more accurate? Isn't this intensely religious? Could any program short of a monastery be more religious than this?

Step 12: *"Having had a spiritual awakening as a result of these steps, we tried to carry this message to others, and to practice these principles in all our affairs."*

Is a "spiritual awakening" different from religious conversion? If so, in what ways? If not, and the awakening occurred "as a result of these steps," is not the program a religious doctrine of redemption and salvation? If twelve-steppers try to "practice these principles in all our affairs," are they not practicing the religious life? How many overeaters are good candidates for this? If twelve-steppers try to "carry this message to other overeaters," aren't they proselytizing, or witnessing, for an evangelical faith? There is no mention here of trying to dissuade other overeaters from overeating or to help overeaters get whatever else they might choose, but only to "carry this message" (the profoundly religious twelve-step program of Overeaters Anonymous) to others so that they might increase their faith in a Higher Power. After that, as part of their orientation, members are helped by their sponsors or in the group to refrain from overeating.

The above discussion of the OA spiritual healing program could continue, but this much should identify some of the issues that confront overweight people who attend OA. None of the above is really new. These questions have been asked for years by the large majority who have ever attended twelve-step meetings.

A recurring question is, "Wouldn't it be good if OA were to change, to 'lighten up on the God part,' to make concessions to the 'agnostics,' to recognize that everyone, regardless of religious faith or the lack thereof, deserves a chance to get better?" There have been some attempts to accommodate agnostics in twelve-step programs by segregating them into informal groups that meet independently, but no program beyond the twelve steps is provided by AA national offices. There is no alternative literature and no plan for recovery except what interested persons might try to derive from the twelve steps. Some white out "God" and inject other abstracts, like "self" or "wisdom," but the result is always incoherent. Those who attend "We Agnostics" groups are accorded second-class membership in every respect, and one may feel particularly marginal to be an agnostic in OA after reading Chapter 4, "We Agnostics," in *The Big Book*.

An even more relevant question is, "Should OA change?" This writer thinks not. It's fine the way it is for those who are inclined to believe in this way. History has shown clearly that conservative religions flourish while liberal ones die out. The reason for this is that religions depend on a nucleus of "true believers" in an inflexible doctrine for inspiration, leadership, and finances, and to make up the rank and file. When the central doctrines are liberalized to accommodate outsiders, or malcontent insiders, the mainstream members feel betrayed and offended, and leave the fold. The outsiders and malcontents, being good liberals, weren't all that interested in causes in the first place and soon abandon ship with the rest. The organization then shrinks in strength and size to a mere residual of its former stature.

From all the foregoing it can be seen that the ideas and philosophies of RR and OA are mutually contradictory and irreconcilable. It would be inappropriate for one organization to try to support two conflicting philosophies. OA is good for those who embrace its doctrines, and to change to accommodate internal dissent would erode its fundamental principles.

A large segment of our health care system has adopted a stance with regard to overweight that follows the traditional values of AA. The following assumptions are guiding principles for health care programming in every community. They are *irrational* when Maultsby's five criteria, mentioned earlier, are applied. Yet they endure.

Assumptions of the Philosophy of Fatness

1. One must have or have had a weight problem ("be one of us") to be effective in helping overweight persons,
   instead of the more rational viewpoint that fat people are not so different or so complex that one can be understood only by someone with a similar personal background. There is no necessary intrinsic difference between fat and thin people except that our appetites cause us some practical problems.
   This point may seem unimportant at first, but it is a serious error of the eating disorder establishment. It segregates fat people unto themselves, incomprehensible and therefore stigmatized. Friendship and useful information can be provided by anyone.

2. It is so difficult to lose weight and keep it off that group support, external direction, or supernatural aid is required,
   instead of the more rational viewpoint that losing weight and keeping it off are not such difficult tasks when compared to the costs of remaining overweight. Recovery from fatness is no big thing, and can occur with or without outside help. Spiritual healing with prayer and Higher Powers is a meaningful occupation for some religiously inclined fat people but certainly not for everyone. Dependence on a Higher Power to lose weight can be seen as setting it up for failure. Simply eating less allows for a gradual return to physical and mental health among spiritual believers and disbelievers alike, but both groups can benefit greatly from some philosophical reconditioning to minimize the chances of fatness relapse.

3. Because overeaters are fundamentally dependent personalities, substitute dependencies, such as on "God as you understand Him," commercial diet centers, doctors, spouses, and dependency groups are necessary to achieve and maintain a desired weight,
   instead of the more rational viewpoint that overweight people aren't much different from others except in their physical dimensions. Although psychological, emotional, and social problems may certainly be caused by becoming overweight, there are no

such things as "addictive" personalities. Because *emotional dependence* is the chief cause of overeating, recovering persons would best pursue *independence,* not only from food binges but from other dependencies as well.

4. Fat people who express disagreement with the twelve-step program, especially "the God part," are either (a) not quite ready to get really serious about their problems, (b) copping out, (c) making excuses so they can justify further overeating, or (d) misguided, spiritually deficient persons who, if they are able to lose a few pounds, cannot expect to keep them off for long or achieve real happiness in life,
instead of the more rational viewpoint that those who object to spiritual teachings and requirements of faith may be commended for exercising critical judgment. Healthy skepticism is the fundamental strength upon which a recovery from fatness can be based.

5. Compulsive overeating is a chronic condition characterized by a daily, lifelong vulnerability to sudden, catastrophic bingeing, so that maintaining a desirable weight requires constant vigilance, self-consciousness, and introspection as well as endless participation in recovery meetings and activities,
instead of the more rational viewpoint that an elegant counterpoint to the spiritual life can be achieved through Rational Recovery; it shows how to take personal responsibility for what is taken into the body and how to avoid fatness relapses, year after year, without supernatural aid, without daily ritual and prayer, without endless meetings with others who also suffer from fatness, and without undue self-consciousness about one's past struggles with fatness. Recovery from fatness is usually an intense struggle at first, but for many it becomes second nature to eat sensibly. Therefore, endless dependency on the initial means of recovery is inappropriate. Each person is the best judge of when recovery from fatness is complete, although he or she may consider the viewpoint of experienced persons in the RR group. Losing weight and maintaining a desirable weight are matters of self-interest, and the locus of emotional and behavioral control is found within.

6. Fat people are obliged to become better people,

instead of the more rational viewpoint that fearless moral inventories (FMI's), while commendable in some respects, are simply not relevant to recovery from fatness. A fearless inventory of self-defeat focusing on the irrational self-sentences that perpetuate the fatness relapse cycle would seem more appropriate for those whose lives are difficult to manage because of fatness. Eating correctly is better than overeating, but one's ethical behavior and moral attitudes are matters separate from recovery from fatness. We do not lose weight to become better people; we do so because we selfishly want more good out of life.

7. Overeating is a symptom of an underlying, practically universal disorder called "the addictive process." The addictive process is a reflection of one's spiritual deficiencies and one's character defects. Those character defects and spiritual deficiencies also underlie many other "sins"—gambling, alcoholism, overspending, "excessive" sexual lusting, shoplifting, masturbating, child-beating, or even experiencing strong moods or emotions,

instead of the more rational viewpoint that overeating is simply a symptom of fatness and the focus of recovery is narrowly defined as the return to physical and mental health that accompanies correct eating. Intriguing research data strongly suggest that overweight is sometimes genetically transmitted and is in no way restricted to those who are morally or spiritually deficient, or without belief in things supernatural.

8. Those closely associated with overeaters are almost always "codependents" who are contributing to the problem,

instead of the more rational viewpoint that it's tough living with a fat person who is self-hating and unhappy, and dealing with a fat mate or family member requires some tough decisions. The prefix "co-" adds nothing to the meaning of the word "dependent," and in fact *obscures* its meaning with an antitherapeutic effect. It is good to recognize one's emotional dependency on a fat person, but one need not come to view himself or herself as spiritually deficient, sick, or "codependent" because of his or her present or past circumstances. Instead, those who are in close relationships with overweight people may be SOdependent on those people for various kinds of fulfillment that they become disturbed and act in self-defeating ways.

9. The desire to think independently and be in control of one's life and destiny is one of the character defects that causes the "addictive process" and "codependency,"

instead of the more rational viewpoint that just the opposite is so. Those characteristics are the chief means by which one may achieve stable weight loss. "Codependency" and "the addictive process" seem to be variations on the theme of original sin.

10. Confession of personal shortcomings and error is intrinsically good and therapeutic,

instead of the more rational viewpoint that confession in itself has little value, and actually perpetuates dependency ideas of guilt and the need for external approval.

11. Fat people are overweight because of some deep, underlying psychological disorder that causes them to regain weight every time they lose some,

instead of the more rational viewpoint that the problem more likely has to do with poor impulse control and low frustration tolerance, neither of which is usually a symptom of an underlying disorder. Happily, a modest effort at improving in these areas may be all that is needed to achieve substantial, durable weight loss. The only "deep" problem that seems common among fat people is their tendency to rate themselves as human beings according to the degree of approval from others, according to their successes and failures, and according to their physical dimensions. Even here, the application of one's native intelligence to the process of rational thinking as described throughout this book may cut deeply into the relapse cycle. But even more importantly, regardless of your degree of success or failure in losing weight, you'll feel better about yourself!

APPENDIX C

RATIONAL RECOVERY® FROM SEXUAL ABUSE

by Jack Trimpey, L.C.S.W.; Director, Rational Recovery Systems

In the past few years there has been a surge of public attention given to persons who believe that as children they had sexual contact with an adult. Hundreds of books have been written seeming to prove that childhood sexual experience produces defective adults with specific emotional and behavioral disorders. As current thinking goes, these "dysfunctional" adults are in need of a cleansing therapeutic experience, usually along the lines of the twelve steps of Alcoholics Anonymous, to gain a grasp on effective living.

In current practice, this therapeutic experience is a past-oriented, "uncovering" process wherein the client is encouraged to "think back" to the time when the molestation occurred and call forth or elicit emotions associated with that scene, such as fear, disgust, revulsion, helplessness, abandonment, anger toward the absent parent for not providing protection, and so on. In individual or group sessions, victims of remote molestation are urged to ventilate these "pent-up" or "stuffed" emotions with the idea that to express them is a way to drain off inner turbulence. In this context, emotions are regarded as existing in their own right, as inner entities to be managed through metaphysical maneuvers in the office setting. Hurtful feelings are sometimes said to be experienced by one's "inner child," and this imaginary child entity is then pampered through regressive psychodramatic techniques, such as toting a stuffed toy. The result of this "working through," in conjunction with spiritual guidance, usually from a nurturing, female therapist who may have a similar background, is said to result in a more peaceful and accepting stance in life.

There is an interesting twist on current sexual dysfunction practices when one cannot remember an actual incident of sexual contact with a parent or other adult but who nevertheless suffers other signs of "codependency," such as worrying too much, feeling too responsible for others, wondering what "normal" family life is like, or simply feeling that life is not rewarding enough. Indeed, anyone who has only vague memories of childhood *in general* is regarded as probably traumatized, probably sexually. Very often, she (most adult victims of remote molestation are female) is assured that because certain "symptoms" are now present, it can almost certainly be assumed that sexual abuse was present in the childhood home. Drawing on psychoanalytic notions of repression and the primal scene, some current therapies are not deterred by the absence of a recollection of sexual contact, but simply assume that these memories are "too painful" to be remembered and will eventually emerge as one proceeds with a program of transpersonal and spiritual growth, as though "peeling an onion." It is assumed that with continued delving and prodding the adult "victim" of childhood sexual abuse will eventually remember the catastrophic circumstances from which stem the above-mentioned "symptoms." Quite often the victims/clients dramatically achieve these recollections during group sessions while others are also generating imagery of sexual victimhood decades ago.

The growing attention to adult victims of remote child sexual abuse signifies a significant change in counseling theory and in our culture. What has emerged in current practice is a new theory of personality development that applies mainly to females, one that traces patterns of adult feminine emotional and behavioral disturbances to childhood sexual involvements. To some it appears to be a variation of the belief earlier this century that masturbation is a cause of mental dullness, physical infirmity, and moral degeneracy. It is widely believed that there is such a disease as "sexual addiction" among incesters, molesters, and other perpetrators of sexual abuse that is transmitted by traumatic conditioning when one has sexual contact with some adult as a child. This dubious assumption may be called "The Vampire Theory," which predicts that victims of perpetrators will become perpetrators. Statistics showing that perpetrators were often once victims of sexual abuse themselves are cited frequently, while little data seem to be available about people who were molested and, perhaps less interestingly, did *not* later develop problems.

Because of the intense grass-roots and media interest in the spicy topics of incest and child molestation, consumers of counseling services would do well to evaluate these claims objectively, clearly if one has actually been molested as a child, but especially if one cannot recall ever having had sexual contact with a parent or other adult. Some kinds of sexual activity (masturbation, playing doctor, adolescent heterosexual and homosexual forays, etc.) are a normal part of growing up, and the gravity now assigned to "molestation" seems exaggerated in an objective context and more a reflection of current social trends than of scientific and clinical findings.

In Rational Recovery we are coming into contact with increasing numbers of individuals who attribute their present patterns of emotional disturbance and self-defeat to having been molested as children. Our culture defines child molestation as "the worst thing there is," even though many of those who were molested tend to disagree.

A rational viewpoint, however, is that while it is *unfortunate and inappropriate* when a child is drawn into sexual activity with an adult, it is clearly not a terrible, catastrophic event that must necessarily result in long-term or even transitory maladjustment. When the molestation is forced or coercive, we may say that it is more than just *unfortunate and inappropriate*—it is *frightening* to the child, and possibly *painful* as well. In the context of our culture, the child may very well be *stigmatized* and feel *guilt and shame,* and when puberty passes, the experienced youngster may be *more promiscuous* than others of her own age. This may lead to more *deviant behavior,* especially when the parents are inadequate in the broad parental role, and when the child harbors a *resentment* toward the same-sex parent for "allowing" the sexual abuse to occur. All of the above observations support the desirability of firm social deterrents to incestuous and pedophilic sexual activity.

Among adults who were molested years or even decades before, the issue can be seen in the light of reason; incidents of childhood sexual abuse need not attain the status of personal tragedy. Counselors and therapists have a responsibility to avoid sensationalizing ancient history among their clients and may apply the REBT paradigm to adult victims of remote child molestation. Four irrational ideas are listed below, along with their rational and therapeutic opposites. These concepts will very likely have therapeutic value when understood by persons who were, or who suspect that they were, molested as children. (The reader is referred to the plethora of literature from the Institute for Rational-Emotive Therapy, 45 East 65th Street, New York, NY 10021, for further reading and study.)

1. My emotions exist independently within me and are somehow forced on me by other people or by external events, past or present,
instead of the rational idea that any feeling or emotion I have is being caused by a *conscious* thought I am having. Human beings feel the way they think and therefore have considerable control over the emotions they experience. By working energetically to discover certain irrational beliefs in my own thinking, I may obtain relief from painful, long-standing conflicts.

2. Certain acts are intrinsically wicked and awful, and those who engage in them are awful, wicked people who should be blamed, condemned, and punished,
instead of the rational idea that while some acts are inappropriate, antisocial, harmful, and unfair, I can come to accept anything that does not kill me. Sexual acts are not intrinsically bad or wicked, but may occur in contexts that are inappropriate, antisocial, harmful, and unfair. If I participated in incestuous behavior as a child, that has no bearing on my self-worth today, or even back then. The adult who molested me was certainly stupid, intoxicated, maladjusted, or irresponsible, but that doesn't make him or

her into an awful, wicked person whom I must now moralistically condemn. By refusing to blame, I can put past issues to rest.

3. The past is a powerful, all-important determinant of my present sorrows and disturbances, and childhood sexual activities are inherently destructive in nature,
   instead of the rational idea that I now feel what I now think. Although I may habitually think how awful it is today that my past was unhappy, I can also see that the past is now only a memory and I can make of that anything I choose. I have no control over my past, but I have enormous control over my present fears, resentments, shame, and guilt. Sexual experiences of children appear more benign and incidental rather than having paramount implications in later psychological development.

4. To feel worthwhile, I must be loved and accepted, and I must also be competent and intelligent in every way,
   instead of the rational idea that because I am an adult, I will concentrate on my own self-respect rather than the respect of others, and I will find far more pleasure in loving than in being loved. Since nothing I can do can prove or disprove my inherent worth, I will assert my own self-worth simply because it feels better. Mine is the final word here, and nobody can stop me from thinking lovingly of myself at all times.

Conclusion

If you were molested as a child, you may or may not have enjoyed it. Either way, the experience has no bearing on your intrinsic worth as a human being and little if any direct bearing on your present adult problems. Whatever trauma you may have felt back then is only a memory today. If you feel stress when you recall an incestuous experience, you are likely blaming and condemning the perpetrator, yourself, or both. If you can't remember much about your childhood, relax; most other people can't either. If you cannot recall an incestuous experience, then none likely occurred. If it did occur, it doesn't really matter now. Blaming yourself or others for being imperfect is a logical error, for everyone is fallible in many respects. With this awareness, you may stop blaming and start living.

Summary

The social moralism of the 1980s has brought an accentuated interest in sexual victimhood. New practices based on a hybrid of Freudian psychology and transpersonal twelve-step concepts have emerged. Unhappy people, mostly women, are viewed as victims and encouraged to blame a broad spectrum of adult problems on past sexual injustices, both real and imagined. Rational-emotive behavior therapy, as self-help or through a professional counselor, may provide an elegant and efficient resolution to conflict that is related to remote molestation.

Criteria for Vigorous Mental Health

THE INSTITUTE FOR RATIONAL-EMOTIVE THERAPY

1. **Self-interest**
    To be true to oneself and not masochistically sacrifice oneself for others, though at times choosing to offer whatever help one can.
2. **Self-direction**
    To assume responsibility for one's own life, though at times choosing to seek the help of others. Willing to take risks.
3. **Tolerance**
    To grant fully to others the right to be wrong, with no attempt to control anyone. Forgiveness.
4. **Acceptance of uncertainty**
    To accept fully the self-evident fact that we live in a world of probability and chance, with no certainties.

5. **Flexibility**

   To remain intellectually flexible, to be open to change at all times, and to choose appropriate behavior for varying circumstances.

6. **Scientific thinking**

   To be objective, rational, and scientific, and to apply the laws of logic and the scientific method.

7. **Involvement**

   To be absorbed vitally in something outside oneself, whether embodied in people, things, or ideas.

8. **Self-acceptance**

   To be glad to be alive; to like oneself just because one is alive and not to equate one's worth with outside achievements or the approval of others.

9. **Freedom from superstition**

   To think for oneself and to make decisions based on reasonable expectations, not on any fatalistic ideas or on the presence of supernatural influence.

Now that you've read
Taming the Feast Beast

To obtain additional copies of *Taming the Feast Beast*, contact Delacorte Press (1-800-223-6834; ask for Special Sales). To order self-help materials, write to Lotus Press, Box 800, Lotus CA 95651. Discounts are available for book dealers and for local RRS projects. You may also call Rational Recovery Systems at (916) 621-2667 or (916) 621-4374.

An expanding line of books on chemical and other dependencies is available, as well as audio and video productions for use in your home or agency. Groups are forming in most American cities. You may call RRS for information on local groups or to seek assistance with starting up new local projects focusing on fatness, alcohol or drug dependency, or other problems of daily living.

INDEX